I0426599

The Ultimate BDSM Resource Book

by Sir Bamm!

This book is dedicated to all of the people who have come before me in alternative lifestyles and have paved the way for this to even be possible. Some of the groups that have earned my respect in that manner are TALON, SSCN, Black Rose, SAADE and JANUS.

This is also for those people whom I admire from those groups, and others, including Malfait, TigerLily, Truth or Dare, slavette, Spinoza, Sir Scott, Victoria Lashes & Master Jam from SSCN, which I feel the most a part of; Ms. Siren, Ambrosio, Lady Caroline, Johnan, lusttwench & Officer Wes from the Austin/San Antonio area; pix, out of SEO; and all those lovely ladies throughout the years - my teens, my military life and beyond, who said, "I like it" to me. All of which has made me who I am today and made me comfortable doing What It Is That We Do.

Introduction

Originally I had planned on creating a web site. Over the course of gathering this material I realized I needed to put it in a book (and make it available on Kindle) so it could more easily be referenced, no matter where it's needed.

In the beginning I was only interested in making a bio and ad. As time went on I realized that in order to write about me, I needed to write about all the things that make up who I am. My life is so "pistachio", that sometimes I think that when I really want to get kinky I need to have vanilla sex!

My feeling is that there are numerous web sites and books that have a lot of great information. However, with the people that I know and the things that I've experienced, I knew that I could make this into a book that contained just about all the information you would ever need, on the subject of What It Is That We Do.

I made a lot of my own dungeon furniture, including a St. Andrews cross, a sub chair, 2 spanking benches, and numerous other toys. I am a single tail Master, given the title, "Expert" with both the 3 foot and the 4 foot signal whip. I have given demonstrations and presentations on signal whips, dungeon monitoring and other topics, all across the US.

I was introduced to the scene while I was in the military. I met a lady who was into BDSM and we experimented. After my honorable discharge and us going our separate ways I didn't know that there were other people like us, so I kept my interests to myself until my first marriage.

My first wife and I would experiment mixing drugs and sex; and after the drugs started affecting the sex, we needed much more intense things just to feel the sex.

When I stopped doing the drugs I thought that I didn't need BDSM anymore, but early in my recovery I met a girl who was also interested in kinky sex. She and I experimented a lot, and after 2 years of switching I found what I wanted and have been Dominant ever since. That was in 1985.

In the time since, I've had a number of submissives, one or two slaves, and a few vanilla relationships. When one of my many relationships ended, one of the last things this particular lady said before leaving was, "Now you can go back to doing those disgusting things that you like to do!"

And I did. Although I had been involved with other non-organized SM groups, my first experience with an SM organization was with the Triangle Munch Group. I met lots of like-minded people in a strictly vanilla atmosphere. While going there, I was introduced to Le Chevalier Malfait. He told me about TALON (the Triad Area Leather Oriented Network). A short time later, while discussing play socials and BDSM groups, Malfait and I came up with the idea for SSCN, (the Safe, Sane, Consensual Network, pronounced, "scene").

Over the years I held different positions within different organizations that I was involved with. I was the NCSF (National Coalition for Sexual Freedom) liaison for one, the DM Supervisor for another, and on the Election Committee for another. I also became an active member of a Dominant's group. Soon after joining that group I became their Chief Security Officer and DM Captain and a mentor in their Mentors Program.

Other things I got involved in included starting a "Train the Trainers" program, an "Escort Service" to walk people that require escorts to their cars after munches, parties and other events; and to form a "security team" to help out wherever the need exists, both inside and outside of alternative lifestyle groups.

If you'd like to know more about What It Is That We Do, if you or your group would be interested in having me do a presentation – either from this book or something else – to do a book signing, to hand me your submissive checklist or if you just have a question or comment, feel free to contact me at SirBamm@SirBamm.com.

I promise to answer all emails, eventually. Please have patience.

Table of Contents

Beginning Training

The following is taken from a presentation given on March 9, 2002. It was given to a Dominants-only group, but the information below is a good starting point for both Doms/Masters and subs/slaves. Note: "Dom" or "Dominant" will be used to mean Dominant, Top and/or Master, "sub" or "submissive" will be used to mean submissive, bottom and/or slave. Developing sub/slave Training Programs:

Opening Statement:
It is an awesome responsibility when someone asks you to train them. Novice Dominants often jump at the chance to prove their prowess without thinking about the time commitment and the entire scenario. This often leads to a mismatch in personalities and expectations. These undetected mismatches lead to training disasters, hurt feelings and tarnished reputations.
In training situations, the Dominant holds the primary responsibility. Part of taking responsibility as a principle trainer is knowing what your personal expectations are. What, exactly, do you want to get out of the situation, then clearly communicating these expectations to the submissive.
Present these expectations in early discussions and negotiations. It should be restated in the form of a written training contract.
So, ask yourself two questions:
1) Am I willing to train for training sake?
2) What do I want to get out of this?
Know what your expectations are before entering into a training contract.

Training Phases:
Submissive training can be broken down into two phases: The Assessment Phase and the Training Program.
The Assessment Phase determines:
1) If You want to train a particular sub
2) The answers gathered dictate the overall direction and structure of the training program.

Assessments:

Assessing Tendencies:

It is equally important to determine the expectations and/or natural preponderance of the submissive. Some subs are hesitant to share this information. If they are attracted to You, they may not want to jeopardize the chance to get to know You better. Some honestly won't know what to expect from a training session.

The following is a technique presented in Miss Abernathy's books. Using simple question/answer quizzes can help reveal tendencies. They aren't always 100% accurate, but for the most part they are revealing and useful.

Assessing Obedience & Willingness:

Require written assignments. Make sure these assignments have a clear completion deadline. If a sub/slave won't obey or work with You or complete the assignments by a reasonable deadline, they will never make it through a serious training program. Following directions is a critical part of any training and the written assignment exercises reveal their willingness to comply. If they fail consistently, do not go forward with the training. This requirement will save You hours of wasted time and energy.

The first three assignments:

1) Start with Miss Abernathy's Quiz
2) 3 Minute Quiz
3) start a slave's journal.

Assessing Openness:

Immediately place the trainee under a full disclosure policy. Under this rule You test the ability of the submissive to be open and honest. It is also an information gathering tool for structuring training and play.

Use this carefully. Depending on the type of training, require an accounting of sexual preferences (monogamous/poly relationships), fantasies, past encounters in the BDSM world, an accounting of things that have gone wrong and things that have gone right. At this juncture You are getting an idea of fears, limits and determining strengths.

It is equally important to know both spoken limitations and physiological limitations. This may come out in intimate discussions.

Risks

Assessing Health Risk:

Never embark on a training program of this type without assessing health risks to You or Your trainee. Sit down and have a heart to heart talk about health issues.

Assessing Work Risk:

If a submissive is employed, be sure to look at the impact such a training program will have on the trainee's work environment. Can the sub play in public or attend D/s affairs in the local area? Is there a danger that being "outed" would jeopardize their livelihood?

Assessing Home Life:

Is the sub married, does the spouse or significant other know about the sub's interest in D/s? Does the sub's "vanilla" friends now about the D/s interest and does s/he share his/her experiences with them? If the neighbors discovered the D/s interest, would there be repercussions?

Assessing Outside Professional's Influences:

Is the sub working with a spiritual counselor, therapist or psychologist? Are these professionals aware of, and accepting of, the D/s interest?

Assessing Limits and Range:

It's important to get an idea of the range and limits of Your play partner.

Training Contracts:
By the time You have finished this type of assessment You have an idea if You want to work with this trainee. Now is the time to consider the depth and time frame that You will spend with someone.

The Training Program:
Here, we begin use the information gathered from the assessment phase. Divide the programming into two categories:
1) Basic Training
2) Advanced Training

Basic Training is meant to lay a foundation of expectations, protocol and rituals to focus the submissive on the Dominant's needs and style of SM.

Basic Training:
1) sub/slaves Presentation - establishing how a submissive will behave toward You and Oothers.

Forms of Address:
    1) How to address and communicate with You
    2) Forms of addressing others
    3) silent communication
       Forms of Service:
    1)How are You to be served under different conditions
    2) High protocol, moderate protocol, scene etiquette or relaxed service
    3) Answer - When, where, how
       Forms of Posture
    How to handle Yourself within a situation

2) Levels of Service:
This is dictated by what it is You want from a situation. Is housekeeping an issue? Laundry? Sexual service? Do You micromanage? Any answer is appropriate.

Mindfulness - No matter what the level of service, it should be done with mindfulness toward the Dominant. Create a time limit for chores and assignments to be completed. Start off with a rigid schedule. Train how You expect services to be performed. If You haven't trained properly, then it is Your fault if something isn't done to Your satisfaction.   Give clear instructions about all areas of training.

3) Playfulness:

Our lifestyle is about naughty fun and decadent behavior. Be serious when it's time to be serious and have fun when it's time to have fun.

Have sexual fun

Create fantasies and explore the limits that have been set. Initiate new play slowly and keep a sense of humor. If things don't work out, laugh about it and discuss it.

4) Begin to establish trust and limits by being consistent in Your training techniques.

Dom's Quiz:

I am interested in:

Rate 0-5   Item

___   A House Servant - Someone to clean, cook or care for your house

___   A Sex Partner - sex slave - no expectations about future relationship

___   A Personal Assistant - A personal Maid or Valet

___   An Escort - A companion for events and travel

___   Trained or Training

Miss Abernathy's sub Quiz:
Taken from *"Training With Miss Abernathy: A Workbook for Erotic Slaves and Their Owners"* by Christina Abernathy

Exercise: Imagine you are a live-in slave, serving your ideal Dominant. What would your life be like?

Choose the answer that most closely fits your dream.
1. At 6 a.m. I am suddenly awakened by...
a. Mistress's bell.
b. Mistress's foot.   .
c. the alarm clock.
d. the wake-up call.

2. It's time to get dressed. I am dressed in...
a. my uniform.
b. nothing.
c. an apron.
d. a suit.

3. If it's a busy day. I spend the morning...
a. mending Master's riding breeches.
b. pleasuring Master.
c. cleaning the hall closet.
d. attending Master as he tours the city.

4. Time for lunch! I eat...
a. in the sitting room.
b. off Mistress's boot.
c. whenever I get a minute.
d. in a nice little cafe Mistress likes.

5.The best thing about being a slave is...
a. being close to Master.
b. the sex.
c. feeling useful.
d. experiencing new things.

6. My strong point is...
a. my knowledge of fashion.
b. my sex appeal.
c. my organizational skills.
d. my people skills.

7. The hardest part of being a slave is...
a. finding time to keep myself looking good.
b. getting my intellectual needs met.
c. the details, all the little details.
d. being on show all the time.

8. After dinner...
a. Master reads the paper while I polish his shoes.
b. we retire to the boudoir.
c. I do the dishes.
d. we're off to the theater with the Joneses.

9. Time for bed. I must...
a. lay out Mistress's outfit for tomorrow.
b. make myself available in case Mistress wants a massage.
c. review tomorrow's menu.
d. get some sleep after pleasuring Mistress. I've got to look my best.

10. I dream about...
a. being allowed to accompany Master on a drive.
b. the day Master lets me masturbate for him.
c. a nice long bubble bath and an intimate dinner out with Master.
d. just staying home one weekend and relaxing.

Miss Abernathy's Scoring System:
The questionnaires' answers point to tendencies.
A's - Service oriented
B's - Sex Servitude

C's - Personal Assistants
D's - Escorts
Add up the A's, B's, C's and D's and you have tendency ranges.

If you chose mostly (a) answers, you may be a good body servant (lady's maid or valet). You value intimacy with the dominant above all else. You are aware of the importance of your physical appearance, and you like to help others look their best. You like personal attention from the dominant and are proud of any trust s/he places in you.

If you chose mostly (b) answers, you are probably most interested I in being a sex slave. You are a highly sexual person with considerable g stamina, and you pride yourself on your sexual technique. While most slaves enjoy some sexual attention, the erotic side of slavehood is what you enjoy.

If you chose mostly (c) answers, you are best suited to be a housekeeper and/or cook. You are very organized and have considerable management skills. You are comfortable dealing with visitors but are you're just as happy behind the scenes.

If you chose mostly (d) answers, you want to be an escort. You have an attractive personality and excellent communication skills. You enjoy meeting new people and serving in public. You don't mind if some people think you're the Dominant's lover; the two of you know the truth about your relationship. Besides, you're very discreet.

Now, of course there will be a mix of answers. Secondary scores are also important.

Three Minute Quiz:
This exercise is used to reveal initial impressions and limitations. It does not mean that these stay that way or that they are intended to be serious blocks for You. Have the sub write out the

first answer she thinks of within a 2 to 3 minute time frame. They have to finish the entire quiz.

I am most proud of _____
My favorite book is _____
When I'm alone I like to _____
I've had a hard time getting over _____
The thing I like best about myself is _____
The one thing I can't stand is _____
I have a right to _____
I am most ashamed of _____
I'm not sure that I can _____
My spiritual life is best described as _____

Health Questionnaire:
Do you have any dietary restrictions?
Are you allergic to anything? (Scene materials as well as common allergies)
Do you wear contact lenses or glasses? Dental bridges or hearing aids?
Do have any injuries that can keep you from service or play type training? (Neck, back, knee injuries)
Do you have any ongoing illnesses or chronic problems? What type of medications or treatments do you take for these?
Make a list of all the vitamins, herbal or nutritional supplements your take?
When was your last blood test and physical? Will you be willing to take a blood test or physical?
Do you use recreational drugs (including alcohol or tobacco)? What? How Often?
Do you have any addictions or are you struggling with an addiction?
Are you recovering from an addiction? Are you clean and/or sober? How long?
Have you suffered from abuse as a child? As an adult? (Physical, verbal, psychological, sexual, spiritual)
If so, are there any triggers that can cause you trauma now?

Do you abuse others, or have abused others, in the past? How have you addressed these problems?
Have you ever had any type of sexually transmitted disease? How was it, or is it, being treated?

Another Questionnaire:
Below is a list that I gathered from information requested from My good friend Officer Wes' petition for a slave/leather boy. I have changed things where appropriate. I did not expect that petitioners answer every single question when responding to this questionnaire, but it seemed like a good place to start to see how much interest they really had and to give Me an idea of what they were like. If you would like to answer this questionnaire, please look through My web site before responding, so you have an idea of what I am interested in. It was not part of the original presentation, but I felt it was appropriate to add at this juncture.

Name (first, middle, last)
Address
If the above is not an Austin-area address, can you come to Austin on a once- or twice-monthly basis?
If not, please explain any limitations (financial inability, care taking commitment, etc.)
Phone number
Date of birth
Highest education completed.
Religious upbringing & current spiritual preference.
What do you seek in a Master/slave relationship?
What are some of your favorite sexual fantasies? Give Me the broad overall picture.
Outside of work and sexual interests, what leisure activities do you enjoy (movies, sports, games, etc.)?
What brings you the most emotional joy?
Do you enjoy any domestic activities in particular (cooking, gardening, laundry, etc.)?
Do you have any particular creative talents?
What would you bring to My family?

Do you have a problem with calling your Master "Sir" at all times?

After a relationship has begun, are you willing to express your situation, distresses, and reservations when asked?

Do you live with someone?

If so, what is the nature of this relationship?

Is there any reason why you would not be able to commit 100% as a slave (past, present or future reason)?

Race

Height

Weight

Gender

Color of eyes

What do you think is your best physical feature?

Include a photo, and the approximate date it was taken, when you respond.

Do you smoke? If so, how much?

Do you drink? If so, how much? How often?

Do you use prescription drugs? If so, what?

Do you use illegal drugs?

Are you disease free?

Do you have any mental problems (including bipolar disorder, manic/depressive)?

Have you been -- or are you being -- treated for depression?

Do you have any disabilities (visible or invisible)?

Do you have any physical limitations which might affect activities? (For example, a bad back might affect work assigned. Sinus problems/nose congestion might impact how you respond to having your mouth gagged.)

Are you allergic to any medications, foods, animals, plants or anything else?

Are there any other health concerns that I haven't touched on?

What is your living situation (own, rent, etc.)?

Type of employment (full time, part time, unemployed)?

What do you do?

Normal work schedule

Do you own a car?

When would you be available to visit with Uus?
List any other subjects or topics you feel are relevant to this questionnaire.

submissive Training
1) Start training your submissive early on. While old "dogs" can be taught new tricks, what's learned earliest, is often learned quickest and easiest. Moreover, the older the "dog", the more bad habits will likely need to be "un-learned". When it comes to raising and training a submissive, an ounce of prevention is certainly worth a pound of cure!

2) Train your submissive gently and humanely, and whenever possible, teach him/her using positive, motivational methods. Keep obedience sessions upbeat so that the training process is enjoyable for all parties involved. If training your sub is a drudgery, rev things up a bit, and try the "play training" approach: incorporate constructive, non-adversarial games (such as "Go Find", "Hide 'n' Seek", retrieving, etc.) into your training sessions.

3) Does your sub treat you like "hired help" at home? Does s/he treat you like a human gymnasium when you're sitting on the furniture? Does s/he beg at the table? Jump up on visitors? Demand your attention by annoying you to death? Ignore your commands? How well your submissive responds to you at home affects his/her behavior outdoors as well. If your submissive doesn't respond reliably to commands at home (where distractions are relatively minimal), s/he certainly won't respond to you properly outdoors where s/he's tempted by other things.

4) Avoid giving your submissive commands that you know you cannot enforce. Every time you give a command that is neither complied with nor enforced your submissive learns that commands are optional.

5) One command should equal one response, so give your submissive only one command (twice max!), then gently enforce it. Repeating commands tunes your submissive out (as does nagging) and teaches your submissive that the first several commands are a "bluff". For instance, telling your submissive, "Sit, sit, sit, sit!", is neither an efficient nor effective way to issue commands. Simply give your submissive a single "Sit" command and gently place or lure your submissive into the "sit" position, then praise or reward.

6) Avoid giving your submissive combined commands which are incompatible. Combined commands such as "Keep quiet and answer Me" can confuse your submissive. Using this example, say either, "Keep quiet" or "Answer Me". The command, "Keep quiet and answer Me" simply doesn't exist.

7) When giving your submissive a command, avoid using a loud voice. Even if your submissive is especially independent or unresponsive, your tone of voice when issuing an obedience command should be calm and authoritative, rather than harsh or loud.

NOTE: Many Dominants complain that their submissives are "stubborn", and that they "refuse to listen" when given a command. Before blaming the submissive when s/he doesn't respond to a command, one must determine whether or not:
a) the submissive knows what the Dominant wants
b) s/he knows how to comply
c) s/he is not simply being unresponsive due to fear, stress or confusion.

8) Whenever possible, use your submissive's name positively, rather than using it in conjunction to reprimands, warnings or punishment. Your submissive should trust that when s/he hears his/her name or is called, good things happen. his/her name should always be a word s/he responds to with enthusiasm, never hesitancy or fear.

9) Correct or, better yet, prevent the (mis)behavior, don't punish the submissive. Teaching and communication is what it's all about, not getting even with your submissive. If you're taking an "it's-you-against-your sub, whip 'em into shape" approach, you'll undermine Yyour relationship, while missing out on all the fun that a motivational training approach can offer. Additionally, after-the-fact discipline does NOT work.

10) When training One's submissive, whether praising or correcting, good timing is essential. Take the following example: You've prepared a platter of hors d'oeuvres for a small dinner party, which you've left on your kitchen counter. Your submissive walks into the room and smells the hors d'oeuvres. s/he air-sniffs, then eyes the food, and is poised to grab one off the platter before it's served. This is the best, easiest and most effective time to correct your submissive: before s/he's misbehaved, while s/he's thinking about stealing the food.

11) Often, Dominants inadvertently reinforce their submissive's misbehavior, by giving their submissive lots of attention (albeit negative attention) when they misbehave. Needless to say, if Your submissive receives lots of attention and handling when s/he jumps up on you, that behavior is being reinforced, and is therefore likely to be repeated.

12) Keep a lid on your anger. Never train your submissive when you're feeling grouchy or impatient. Earning your submissive's respect is never accomplished by yelling, hitting, or handling your submissive in a harsh manner. Moreover, fear and stress inhibit the learning process.

Two other items that were included in the presentation, 9 Levels of submission and submissive BDSM checklist, I have not included here because they can be found elsewhere on my web site.

An additional excerpt from another of Siren's submissive Training Workshop (© 2002 Ms Siren) goes on to discuss the intonations of your voice:

The tone of voice is an often used and underestimated powerful element in training your submissive.

Of course you recall one of the most infamous statements in every parent's repertoire, "Don't take that tone with me." Tone of voice expresses mood, intent, meaning and desires of the speaker. Studies indicate that tone of voice is a major contributor in helping us to understand the spoken word, phrase and sentence. Consider the tone of voice attached to the description of sarcasm or using my best "bedroom voice". We take for granted the power of tone of voice, until we see it in action. Consider the seven words in the sentence below.

I didn't say Sally stole that flogger.

The sentence is clear, concise and easy to understand, right? But wait, what does it really mean? Take a moment and reread that sentence out loud... seven times. Each time put an accent on a different word, for instance, I didn't say..., I DIDN'T say..., I didn't SAY....

How many different meanings or expressions of intent did you discover? Seven? You are correct. Because of the use of tone, that one sentence changed meaning seven times. This is an example of why the casually written word is often misunderstood, and the reason tone is so important in getting your message across to others.

The power of intonation has a significant impact when training your submissive, in a positive and less than positive manner. Tone is used appropriately when it is consistent with the circumstances at hand. Consider how you say your submissive's name when you are proud of something they've done. Does that change when you are in a playful mood? An angry mood? A loving mood? When your tone matches the circumstances at hand, trust is developed and maintained. It supports the development of dependability and stability in your relationship.

However, if you use tone inappropriately, if your tone does not match the circumstances at hand, it can create a level of mistrust. For example, you call your submissive with your "bedroom voice" and when they come to you they receive a severe reprimand. They will learn to mistrust that voice of seduction.

Ask yourself some questions to determine if intonation is an area you should improve: Am I using appropriate tone when praising, reprimanding or consoling my submissive? Is my submissive misinterpreting my comments or commands? Does my submissive seem suspicious of my requests? Does my submissive ask, "Now what have I done?" every time I call their name? Do I find our conversations include, "That's not what I meant", "But that's what you said" statements?

"Say what you mean and mean what you say" is an important concept in training your submissive. The use of appropriate intonation is a major contributor in "meaning what you say."

Boundaries

Because of all the talk about people, both Tops and bottoms, crossing boundaries and not knowing what to do when someone crosses their boundaries, with a little help from My good friend Alpha, I put this page together based on information found on both vanilla web sites and leather ones concerning this topic.

Although some of this information is set up for the vanilla world, and meant to be used in work, home, school and extra-curricular athletic activities, these principles work just as well in pistachio settings.

Note: The below information was taken from *Father's World. Advanced Boundary-Setting* by Rinatta Paries. I take no credit for it. Numerous attempts were made to contact the author.

Are you holding back from letting others know where you draw the line, from setting your personal boundaries? The following points may be just the inspiration you need to set your boundaries and start getting more good stuff out of your relationships.

Good, decent people set boundaries.
In fact, the more boundaries you set, the more you are being good to others and yourself. Establishing boundaries makes you a safe person. People know where they stand with you.

Generous people set boundaries.
If you do not have boundaries, you are essentially giving yourself away. With boundaries, you give only what you want, which means you can afford to be generous to more people over longer periods of time.

To be effective, try to relate to others.
If you want people close to you to consistently respect your boundaries, try to understand why they are crossing them. If you

can, make it easy to respect your boundaries by giving them what they need. For example, does your mother call you incessantly because she worries about you? What kind of information can you share with her to make her worry less?

Boundaries allow people around you to grow.
When you set boundaries, it makes others conscious of their behavior. This fosters their own growth. Your boundaries can actually improve other people's lives.

Boundaries help you get more of what you want, and less of what you don't. Boundaries can be used not only to protect you from unwanted behavior, but also to foster behavior you desire and need. Figure out what you need from others to thrive, and then ask for what you want and accept nothing less.

Stick to your guns.
In order for boundaries to be a reality in your life and not just a nice concept, you must be aware and willing to act consistently. You must have a commitment to uphold what is right and true for you.

Practice makes perfect.
Learning how to set boundaries and how to have only what you want in your life takes time and practice. It will feel awkward at first. People may not like what you are saying. But keep practicing and communicating. You will get better, more skilled, and more graceful.

Enjoy the benefits of boundary-setting:
Freedom from fear and pain
Increased self-esteem and self-respect
More respect of and from others
Contribution to the well-being of others' lives
Finally have a life that you love.

Go out and practice. Your life and relationships will blossom from it!

Your Relationship Coach
Rinatta Paries
(c) Rinatta Paries, 1998-2002.

Note: The below information was found at *Skysite*. I take no credit for it. Numerous attempts were made to contact the author.

2 Decisions and 4 Steps by David Burnet, *The Learning Coach* with grateful appreciation to Thomas Leonard & Coach U.

Decisions about boundary setting:
1. Decide what you want and don't want from/with people. A good idea is to do this both in general, and with any person or situation that reveals that more boundaries are needed (you know you need boundaries when you are frustrated, angry, or hurt).
2. Decide to be extremely sensitive about boundaries (enlarge your boundaries), and to be constructive about enforcing them.

Steps to enforce boundaries:
1. Educate or inform people what they are doing. Just inform them in a matter of fact way.
2. If it continues, tell them what you want and don't want, and how you feel about that.
3. If it continues, warn them how you will separate yourself from them &/or their negative behavior, either temporarily (while it continues), or if necessary, permanently.
4. If it continues, distance yourself as you said you would, preferably short term, long term when necessary.

Warnings:
1. Memorize this list, it may be all you can remember, the first few times when you are under pressure and need to enforce

boundaries. Soon, because it works so well, you'll probably learn to do this fairly automatically and well.

2. The first few times you do this, it will be hard for people who already know you, because they aren't used to this. They may over-react. They may also over-react because the first few times you do this you won't be as skillful as after you've practiced this. Happened to me, and I've noticed to other people.

It can be helpful to notify people about what you are learning and doing, ahead of time, and to let them know that you won't be as skillful, at first; you may be heavy handed...but to please be patient and bear with you. It will help you and them, too, to get along better.

Note: The below is taken from *The Compleat Slave* by Jack Rinella (Used with permission). Jack is writing in respect to two specific relationships; however his advice is sound for all boundary setting circumstances:

There are Master/slave relationships that are totally one-sided in terms of control, but they are neither newly-formed, nor of an occasional occurrence. David, brand new in the scene, and without experience or self-confidence, is in no position to jeopardize his permanent family relationships or to be the kind of slave he's not ready to be.

My advice was to meet the guy again but, before starting another scene, tell him they need to talk seriously, and as adults, about limits, fantasies, and reality. In short, David should approach his partner not as a submissive or slave, but as an adult. They need to negotiate in a responsible manner, and delineate exactly what the two of them could and couldn't do.

I advised him to be humble and respectful, but to make himself absolutely clear. It would be better to end the relationship than to continue playing in ways that were unacceptable to one or the other of the partners.

I'm a firm believer that submissives can't abrogate their responsibility. Master or slave, each is supposed to be a reasonable, consenting adult. Neither ought to give up on creating a satisfactory relationship. I will admit that there are relationships where the submissive can and should abrogate all self-will, but I condone it only when that relationship is mutually and fully agreed upon by both parties, without coercion or deceit. I'm all in favor of total obedience, but that occurs only on the fringes of the bell curve. Most S/M is still R&P (Restraint and Pleasure)!

The third recent indication of the need to play responsibly came in the form of a disturbing message on my answering machine. It seems that my friend Bob and a friend agreed to do a cigar-burning scene where the top would burn Bob. I don't know the circumstances of the agreement, but it was negotiated and they played it out.

The next morning Bob was angry to see that he had been badly burned and perhaps scarred for life. The cigar-imposed marks were extremely painful. What might have been a good scene last night was now a really bad one.

In this situation, both top and bottom needed to be more responsible in their respective decisions. I would suggest that their negotiation wasn't explicit enough. Did Bob know there would be scars the next morning? Did the top really want to make permanent alterations to Bob's flesh? When two people agree to a scene they need to know exactly what they're agreeing to. Bob's regrets could have been avoided with just two minutes more of negotiation, or just one minute more of exploration about the effects of playing with cigars.

Regrets are such bad feelings. That's another reason to negotiate responsibly. Once again, I have no problem with a master marking or even scarring a slave for life, but it is probably not appropriate to do it as a part of a one time, one-night scene.

In fact, it may be that the master thought he was doing exactly what Bob wanted. If such is the case, he should have been thoroughly sure. In this negotiation, verbal clues such as, "I'm going to really mark you" would have told Bob what he was in for. It's at that point, too, that Bob would have had the opportunity to say, "stop."

This is certainly a case for mutual responsibility. Perhaps Bob should now say something to his master about that night so that they both can learn from the incident. Bad-mouthing the master to others would not be productive. The unfortunate incident was co-created. Each must bear his fair share of the blame.

Note: The above was taken from pages 34-35 of chapter 3 of Jack's book, *The Compleat Slave* and was used with Jack's permission.

In closing, important things to remember (for both Tops and bottoms):

If you attend a play party, you are expected to know that the other people there might ask you to play. There is a wide variety of play that is possible. In other words, please read and be familiar with the party's rules.

The person who asks is expected to be polite, and to respect the collar of anyone who is collared, or to respect the relationships of other couples or leather families.

If you want to play with the person who asks, you are welcome to say, "Yes."

If you do not want to play with the other person, you are expected to say, "No." If you do not want to play with the other person, but say, "Yes," or do not safe word (if that is what is necessary to prevent unwanted play), then you have not done what is necessary to prevent any further advances and cannot expect that the other person will know what it is that you want.

If you ask someone to play, and they say, "No," you are expected to respect their wishes, and to let the matter drop. Also, be mindful of other people's personal space.

Honest, open and respectful negotiation is almost always welcome. Nonconsensual play is not!

If you agree to the use of safe words (i.e., Green [everything is good, please continue], Red [stop the scene immediately]), you are expected to use them, especially if your status is anything other than Green.

If someone is bothering you, stalking you, continually following you around, or won't take "No" for an answer, or if you even perceive this to be the case, it is quite all right (and even encouraged) for you to use the safeword to stop the advances. Even if you are not in a play area, if a Dungeon Monitor (here after referred to as DM) hears "Red", they will immediately investigate.

Even if you are in a social area, sitting down, minding your own business, if someone bothers you, won't leave you alone or won't go away, and you have told them that you are not interested, say, "Red". Either they will get the hint, or a DM will.

If you say, "No" or "Red" and the person doesn't heed your wishes and no DM hears your safeword, immediately get up and walk to the nearest DM and tell them what is going on. At that point, they will either call for a supervisor or handle the situation themselves, immediately. Immediately, is when the situation needs to be handled. Not later, not tomorrow and not at the next party. And don't be afraid to do it. You had the courage to come to the party, have the courage to talk to the one person who can ensure your safety - the DM.

Scene Etiquette is dynamic and personal. It differs depending on the individual and the situation. Always practice an attitude which fosters courtesy and respect among individuals within the leather community. Being mindful of scene etiquette is paramount.

If you have any concerns, bring them to the attention of a DM, immediately. Telling someone at the next party that someone did something to you at the last party may not get you the desired response.

Do not interfere with any else's scene. Do not invade their scene space. Keep conversation, laughter and comments to a minimum in the play areas. And, do NOT join a scene unless specifically asked to do so!

Comprehensive Dungeon Monitors Guide
© 2008, 2013 by Sir Bamm!

Purpose:
The purpose of this Dungeon Monitor's Guide is to provide members of the BDSM-leather-fetish community with a general guideline to equip them with the basic knowledge and skills required to be a play monitor (hereafter referred to as a dungeon monitor or DM) at an SM event. It is hoped that through education efforts such as this, we, as a community, can continue to grow and become more proficient and professional in our endeavors. This guide was developed to assist in the education of DM's for local events, and therefore includes general rules and standards.

Disclaimer:
The information contained in this guide represents the opinions of various organizations and individuals. The authors, editors, publishers, contributors, and/or distributors of this booklet accept no responsibility or liability for any accident, injury, mishap or incident that may occur to any individual(s) or groups as a result of performing any of the activities described or alluded to herein.

Acknowledgements:
I would like to recognize the following organizations and individuals for their work that enabled this initiative to become a reality:

Reference Information:
Black Rose, Black Rose Board of Directors 1998, Boy Max, BR98 Dungeon Staff, Chris M., David S., Fraizer, Gil Kessler, Jack McGeorge, Joseph Bean, Leather Leadership Conference II, Trish A., Johnan and Bamm!

Special thanks to The BR98 Play Monitors Guide, which served as the basis for the "Danger Signs" reference charts, and Johnan, for the Crisis Intervention essay. To the ARC and FEMA for the list of First Aid support and First Aid kit contents. And to SAADE, SSCN and TALON.

Editors: Bamm! and His! t.

Preface:
Volunteering to be a Dungeon Monitor, or DM, has a great many rewards. Not only do you have a chance to give something back to the community that you play in, but you can also get a lot of personal satisfaction from doing it. There is also a great deal of knowledge to be gained from the experience. Personal satisfaction comes from being able to feel that you are unconditionally helping people, regardless of their background or kink. The giving of your time and energy and knowledge helps others out, just like you were helped out (or wish you were) when you were new to the leather-SM-fetish community. The knowledge you get is not only from the DM course, but also from being able to observe all the various techniques and skill levels of the players at a party. This DM course is designed to give you the basic knowledge of how to be a good Dungeon Monitor, a certification in CPR and First Aid, and a basic knowledge of crisis control and aggression management. These basic skills, along with the things that you already know, and may not even know that you know them, combined with the experience from DM's that are already in place, will give you valuable tools that will be sought out for many years to come. These things also have other benefits, like reduced party admissions to most clubs that you will be available to DM for. We hope you enjoy this course, and learn from it, as much as we have from taking it in the past and teaching it today.

Forward:
Safe, Sane, and Consensual . . . the leather culture creed. In April of 1998, the Leather Leadership Conference II defined SSC as:

"Safe" is being knowledgeable about the techniques and safety concerns involved in what you are doing. Each participant must be informed about the possible risks, both mental and physical.

"Sane" is knowing the difference between fantasy and reality. Knowledgeable and informed consent cannot be given if you are under the influence of alcohol or other drugs.

"Consensual" is respecting the limits imposed by each participant. One of the most easily recognized ways to maintain limits is through a "safeword" - which ensure the bottom/submissive can end the activity at any time with a single word or gesture.

As the Leather Community grows, so does its need to provide education and support for its participants. This support includes an atmosphere where people can explore themselves and D/s-SM. A Play Party or Play Social is by nature, one of those places of exploration, self-education, and support. As such, it is a common function provided by BDSM support groups as well as individuals. Parties attract newcomers and experienced players alike. The level of understanding of scene etiquette, use of equipment, and safety techniques will vary among players. Because of this, the importance of having one or more trained DM's for the event cannot be under-estimated. The safety of the attendees is at stake, as is the reputation of the organizers. The DM fulfills an important role in making the event successful and comfortable. To this end, the DM is a lifeguard (monitoring play space, providing assistance, intervention and instruction if needed); a guide (providing directions, safety equipment, and information); and a cop (enforcing the rules established by the organizers). Participating in an event as a DM is a tough but rewarding job. You have to enforce the rules while maintaining your impartiality toward all participants. It's not always a fun job, but it will always be one of the most important within the scene.

Essentials of play monitoring:

The DM Mission:

The mission of the DM is, simply, to ensure a safe, enjoyable play environment.

Your Duties as a DM:

To attend necessary orientations and training sessions. To be friendly and courteous to all participants. To provide orientation and assistance where appropriate. To supervise all SM activities in the play areas and to take appropriate steps to ensure the safety of all participants. To be familiar with general scene etiquette, specific play rules, and all the individual policies that apply to play; and to enforce these rules and policies. To conduct safety inspections of play areas and equipment and take appropriate corrective action if unsafe equipment is discovered. To ensure that play rules are available to all participants. To maintain a clean and orderly play environment. To report shortages of expendable supplies to the organizers. To monitor play activities for danger signs and substantial breaches of scene etiquette. To assist players with minor injuries as necessary. To ensure that players clean up when a scene is complete.

Safety and Security:

Part of any DM's job may involve safety issues or security issues. One of our duties is that of a police officer. We constantly say it, but there really isn't a lot said about how to go about it. Some of the basics are set out as follows.

Traffic Control:

For whatever reason, there may come a time when directing traffic becomes necessary. Sometimes it is because of the size of the crowd. Sometimes there may have been an accident. Rarely it may be due to a scene caused by a player that needs to be removed from the premises. Regardless of the nature of the reason, if you are not directly involved with the incident, you can be indirectly a part of it, which makes you directly responsible to the safety of the participants. While things are being handled in one area, you may have to stand in another and keep people moving. You may have to keep people away and you may have to keep people back. In all of these instances, remain polite, but firm. Stand your ground and don't spend a lot of time answering questions. Tell people, politely, "I'm not sure, I'll find out for you later". This gives them a sense of importance and will leave you alone to do your job.

Checking ID's:
When working the door for a party, sometimes friends and strangers will "forget" their card or have "lost" it or "left it home". As much as we'd like to accommodate everyone and keep our friends and give our friends a break, for the safety and security and legal aspects that may arise, it is important that we are firm and consistent with everyone. If you are required to have a membership card, than not having one will get you turned away. Period. If waivers are required, then full legal names are required on them. Refusing to sign, incorrectly signing or not using their full legal name will weaken the release of liability. Therefore you must check the waiver to see that it is filled out completely and signed legally and legibly.

Escort Service:
Whenever a person, male or female, feels uncomfortable walking out to their car, it is our job to escort them, if asked. We may be nothing more than company. But sometimes, just being company, puts a person's mind at ease.

Prior to Duty:
Study the event play rules. Study this guide. Be on time for your shift. Familiarize yourself with the event space and equipment. Familiarize yourself with the supplies and the location of supplies. Get a feel for scenes in progress and the mood in general. Check in with the event organizer(s) or DM Supervisor. Get a debriefing from the DM going off-duty. Get your gear ready and on: DM vest (if available) Vest Pack (with flashlight, trauma shears, gloves, CPR masks, pen and whistle).

On Duty:
Patrol the play space with the aim of facilitating a safe and enjoyable time for all - keep an active pattern of movement and deep social interactions to a minimum. You will have another time to interact with others socially. Patrol the entire play space - as the DM, you will have complete access to all play areas. Look - keep your eyes moving. Focus actively but not exclusively on the play. Watch for over-obtrusive voyeurs, alcohol, drunkenness, and over-aggressive come-ons. Watch with impartiality, keeping safety and effectiveness in mind. You can watch for pleasure after your shift is over. Listen - listen for trouble. You may hear something go wrong before you see it. Yelling, screaming, sounds of equipment breaking or collapsing should be investigated immediately. Remember that even happy screaming might disturb others. Loud conversations in play areas should be discouraged. Communicate with other DM's - share impressions of scenes in progress, communicate equipment maintenance information, and confirm whether intervention is necessary or whether the event organizer or DM supervisor should be called. Communicate with Players - provide direction (to restrooms, cleaning supplies, house rules, smoking area, etc.), provide aid (answer questions, stalker complaints, and enforce rules). Good Opening Lines - "Is everything okay?" or "Excuse me, could I be of assistance?" Vocal Tone - calm, professional, friendly, do not be smug or bossy, and do not wag your finger. Enforce House Rules - violations of written play/social rules can and should be enforced without qualm. Monitor for Unsafe Play - watch for violations of house etiquette and if you observe clear violations of house rules or etiquette, you have a clear right to ask for compliance to the rules. Unless the play seems truly hazardous with imminent harm a possibility, you may want to obtain a second opinion from another DM, if available, or the supervisor or organizer. Intervention - make sure that your point of concern has a legitimate basis within the rules. Discreet Intervention - one tactic; get the attention of the top and signal him/her aside. When Intervening - be diplomatic and discreet. Be Fair - explain

your concern to the involved party, point out the area of your concern in the rules. Be Assertive - if the guest is breaking a hard rule, insist that they refrain from doing so. Say you'll call the DM Supervisor or organizer if you can't get your point understood. If the organizer or DM Supervisor overrules your decision, take it in stride and continue your patrol. That rarely happens. Most organizers and DM supervisors trust the judgment of the DM. Either way, do not argue with the organizer or DM Supervisor. Be Firm - be firm with your resolve that the house rules be obeyed. If Problem Persists - intervene again and notify the DM Supervisor. If Violations Continue - suspend the scene.

Operational Procedures Number One Rule: Stay Calm!

Common Medical Problems:
Blood Drawn - Disinfect the wound with an antiseptic wipe and cover with a bandage. Fainting or Near Fainting - lay subject down; cushion head with folded vest or jacket; elevate legs. When subject is feeling better, allow him / her to sit up. Only then offer water or fruit juice for energy.

Other Possible Problems:
Fights and Physical Confrontations - in the extremely unlikely case that a fight breaks out, do not leap into the fray. Use your voice, tell them to stop, call for help. Event organizers will be on their way. Police and Other Official Visitors - be calm and cooperative. If the event is properly run, there won't be a problem. We are out of the norm, but not criminals.

Supplies Available to DM:
First Aid Kit
A good First Aid kit should include, at a minimum, the following items:
1. A brightly colored, lockable toolbox. Lockable in order to keep children out of it.

2. Various types of antibiotic creams and ointments such as Neosporin, Triple Antibiotic Ointment, Bacitracin, Polysporin Powder, Mycostatin Powder

3. alcohol swabs

4. betadine swabs

5. benzalkonium chloride swabs

6. ammonia inhalants

7. About 4 different types of first aid tapes

8. EMS scissors

9. Band-Aids

10. steri-strips, different sizes

11. clear dressings, different sizes

12. applicator swabs

13. emergency thermal blanket

14. wash-up towelettes, or you can use alcohol wash

15. instant activating ice bag

16. tongue depressors

17. latex gloves

18. flashlight, working

19. hydrogen peroxide

20. sterile normal saline

21. various sizes of sterile gauze, both for wrapping and applying over wounds

22. package of 4x4 non sterile gauze, for cleaning and absorbing Sharps Container(s) (if blood play is allowed) Disinfectants Fire Extinguishers Clean Towels Clean Blankets Telephone(s) Radio (if available) Paper Towels Bio-Hazard Rubber Gloves Knife Shears Bolt Cutter Hacksaw

The following information on assembling your own first aid kit is derived from recommendations from the Federal Emergency Management Agency.

A first aid kit should include:
Sterile adhesive bandages in assorted sizes
2-inch sterile gauze pads (4-6)
4-inch sterile gauze pads (4-6)

Hypoallergenic adhesive tape
Triangular bandages (3)
2-inch sterile roller bandages (3 rolls)
3-inch sterile roller bandages (3 rolls)
Scissors
Tweezers
Needle
Moistened towelettes
Antiseptic
Thermometer
Tongue blades (2)
Tube of petroleum jelly or other lubricant
Assorted sizes of safety pins
Cleansing agent/soap
Latex gloves (2 pair)
Sunscreen
Non-prescription drugs
Aspirin or non-aspirin pain reliever of choice
Anti-diarrhea medication
Antacid (for stomach upset)
Syrup of Ipecac (use to induce vomiting if advised by the Poison Control Center)
Laxative
Activated charcoal (use if advised by the Poison Control Center)

The following items should also be included in a kit designed for play party use. Honey packets, sugar gel, or other similar items for use in individuals with low blood sugar Alcohol wipes Extra latex gloves Hand disinfectant Portable sharps container Resuscitation shields Specialized items as determined by local need

Remember - Plan for the worst, and hope for the best

Play Equipment:
Any broken or unsafe equipment should be repaired or marked "DO NOT USE" with a sign placed on the equipment. Be familiar with all equipment to be used / available during play.

Danger Signs:
Things to Watch for:
The following list catalogues a variety of common play mistakes, grouped by the type of scene, that the DM should watch for. Remember your role as a DM is that of lifeguard, helper and guide; not an overzealous school hall monitor. The danger signs are grouped into three categories:

M - Monitor Danger signs rated (M) may or may not be a problem. These involve harmless oversights, mildly risky behavior, or advanced play by experienced players. Make no intervention, but stay alert. Get another DM's opinion if available or contact the event organizer / DM Supervisor if you are in doubt about the scene. There may be a problem brewing.

I – Intervene:
Danger signs rated (I) are situations in which DM intervention is deemed appropriate. This rating does not necessarily mean that a violation of safe or sane play has occurred. Interventions can and should be done for a number of valid reasons: To demonstrate how a technique is performed or how a piece of equipment is used. To inquire about how a scene is being conducted (some players take one-gallon enemas or use wire whips). To inform players about some external circumstance (closing time, the presence of police, etc.). To offer assistance or provide materials to a scene in progress (towels, safe sex supplies, etc.) To share an observation the top may not have noticed (bluing of hands, spilled drink on flogger, etc.). To inform players that they are approaching or have exceeded a safety limit. To be courteous and helpful. The issue may be something the players are too inexperienced to know about. It may be advanced edge play performed by expert players accustomed to

doing it. Satisfy yourself that all is well, help them find a way to do what they want to do safely or ask politely that they refrain from the activity in question.

S - Stop Danger signs so clearly in violation of Safe, Sane and Consensual behavior that they cannot be permitted regardless of circumstance. This does not mean suspend the individual's right to play, but the proscribed behavior must cease and desist. Again, be polite and helpful, but firm. One can't do everything in public.

In Summary:
M means potential trouble to be noticed and monitored.

I means intervention is appropriate, but not necessarily that an activity must cease.

S means a hard limit, and the current activity must stop In general watch for potential risk.

So, the players seem to know what they are doing? If it helps when intervening, point out where the behavior in question appears in this guide.

General Play Space Behavior:
I - Arguments or loud swearing; loud offensive speech involving race, religion or orientation.
I - Bottom weeping, screaming or bothering other people.
I - Bottoms having breathing difficulties; gasping, wheezing or unable to catch breath.
I - Individuals monopolizing play space or equipment.
I - Observers crowding a scene too closely; or getting in the way.
I - Play area is not cleaned before or after a scene.
I - S - Violations of posted house rules,
I or S - According to rule in question.
M - I - Aggressive and persistent stalker-like behavior (M) then (I).

M - I - Drunkenness, belligerence, slurred speech (M) for observers and (I) for players. Keep a close eye out for anyone who appears to be drunk and warn your fellow DM's and organizer(s).
M - I - Excessive noise or screaming (M) then (I).

Play Equipment Safety (Always notify event organizer):
S - Structure, hooks, eyebolts or legs loose.
I - Structure appears unable to support the weight of players.
M - I - Ropes used do not appear strong enough to support the weight (M), if obvious (I).
M - Top has not tested the amount of weight to be supported.

Negotiation and Consent:
S - Ignoring safeword "red".
M - Pushing bottom (or top) too hard to take or give more.

Bondage:
S - Player falls or gets hit on the head.
S - Ropes around neck or collar attached to a high stationary point.
I - Breasts bound tightly causing ballooning.
I - Clips or clamps around the eyes.
I - Standing mummification without spotter.
M - Absence of emergency release tools: knife, shears, bolt cutter or hacksaw
M - Bound player is left alone with no spotter.
M - Collar is too tight to allow free breathing (allow room to insert two fingers).
M - Hands or feet becoming discolored or cool to the touch.
M - Noticeable swelling or redness from bondage or weights.
M - Standing unsupported with ankles bound together - unstable especially with high heels.

Suspension - All Bondage Danger Signs Apply Here Also:
I - Wrist suspension; bondage too tight or too loose, potentially causing nerve damage (room to insert one finger is ideal).

M - Absence of panic snaps at heavy load points.
M - Limbs taut (especially from overhead suspension).

Impact Play:
S - Flogger or whip infringing on other scenes.
S - Hard paddling on the ribs, back, knees or tops of feet or shins.
S - Hard striking on bones or organs, especially kidney, spine, neck or head.
S - Striking bleeding wounds, causing airborne droplets.
S - Striking with the buckle end of a belt.
S - Whip inappropriately long for play space.
I - Whip dragging on dirty floor between strikes.
I - Hard impact on the breasts, especially large breasts.
I - Striking on pre-existing bruises.
M - I - Flogger tips inadvertently wrapping around the body being hit. May leave marks over shoulders, around ribs, outside of hips and side of body away from the one flogging. (M) then (I).
M - Bottom snapping head back sharply when struck.
M - Facial expressions or cries of apparent anguish.
M - Flogger tips dragging on the ground.
M - Paddles or canes are cracked, split or broken.

Breast Play:
I - Breasts bound tightly causing ballooning.
I - Hard impact play on the breasts, especially large breasts.

Wax, Fire and Temperature:
I - Absence of nonflammable drop cloth.
I - Candle flames in the vicinity of curtains or other flammable materials.
I - Absence of wet towel - provide one.
I - Excessive spillage of wax.
M - Mentholated ointments spread over the bound player without soap and water handy.
M - Mentholated ointments placed inside the vagina or rectum.

Electricity:

I - Any direct current electricity (Folsom or OMRON units) used above the waist, or on opposite arms, anything potentially running current through the chest or head.

I - Static electricity used near flammable liquids (alcohol, perfume) and vapors.

I - Violet wand or static electricity used near the eyes.

M - Strong current (cattle prod, stun gun) applied to strong muscle groups.

M - Violet wand or static electricity used on metal jewelry (generates heat).

Genital Play Note: Some players may be "Fluid Bonded" but should still observe safer sex practices in public play space.

S - Blood flow from the vagina or rectum (may need to call 911).

S - Forcing air into the vagina.

I - Bodily fluids on floor or equipment not cleaned up promptly.

I - Fisting without a fresh latex glove and ample lubricant.

I - Moving objects directly from the anus to vagina.

I - Sharing bodily fluids between the players.

I - Sharing toys or objects without changing condoms.

I - Sudden yanking or twisting of testicles.

Cutting or Piercing:

I - S -No first aid kit (I) provide if available, otherwise (S).

I -Antiseptic wipes and dressing are not close at hand.

I - Blood or other fluids on floor or equipment not cleaned up promptly.

I - No sharps container or container not being used, provide one if available.

M - Area of skin to be played with has not been cleaned with alcohol.

Anal Play:

S - Any amount of blood from the rectum.

S - Forcing air into the rectum.

I - Absence of blood cloth, towels, or other enema cleanup supplies.
I - Fisting without a fresh latex glove and ample lubricant.
I - No obvious place for bottom to void after enema.
I - Object for anal insertion does not have a flared base or long handle.

Gagging:
M – I - Gag is not easily removable.
M - Gag with hood.
M – I - Mouth stuffing is not attached to a strap to prevent blocking the throat.
M - Use of a "pump gag" (can over-inflate and block the throat).

Breath Deprivation
M - Bagging or causing bottom to inhale carbon dioxide.
M - More than momentary depravation of air.

Stress and Emotional Danger:
S - Shallow breathing, cold, clammy glassy eyes (possibly endorphin shock).
M - Overly frightened expression.

Crisis Intervention:
Dealing with Non-physical Offenders: Crisis intervention is a way to calm a situation that could result in loud or obnoxious behavior, or even extend to the individual becoming assaultive.

(NOTE: Definition of assault is "unwanted touching").

The possible causes for this type of behavior include, but are not limited to, drinking, anger, relationship issues, lack of proper communication, lack of experience or mental health issues.
If a person starts to display a noticeable change in his or her behavior, such as staring, twiddling fingers, thumbs or hands, walking back and forth absent-mindedly, etc., the DM's should approach the situation in a supportive and non-judgmental

attempt to relieve the tension and try to put the person at ease. If the individual gets to the point where he or she starts to talk back or gets belligerent, it is the DM's job to attempt to take control of the situation by setting rules using a direct and firm approach. If the person has gone into an instinctive behavior of "fight or flight" and has chosen to "fight", the DM Team should first try to take control of the situation, without yet getting physical, to reduce the risk of the offending individual harming himself, the DM's or other group members. If the person has become physical with the DM's, the DM Team or other group members, see "Dealing with Potentially Violent Offenders", below.

Once the person has passed through these phases, whether they have become physical or not, they would normally reach an exhaustion point where the body and the mind become tired and the individual usually begins to regain their composure. At this point he or she would normally begin to feel foolish, silly, embarrassed or apologetic, and it is the DM Team's responsibility to reassure the individual and ease the person back into the "community".

Dealing with Potentially Violent Offenders:
As a DM, sometimes it is important to have to intervene. When approaching someone who needs to be approached, never assume a combative position. Do not wag your finger or raise your voice. Always try to talk in a gentle, calming voice. A good opening line would be "Hi. Can I talk to you?" Or, "Can we talk for a minute?" If someone gets combative, do not stand with your body directly facing them. Always try and stand sideways, giving them less of a target should they decide to throw a fist or foot. It also appears less aggressive if you do not have the appearance of going 'toe to toe' with them. And it is a more powerful position should you need to become physical. Whenever possible, always call for another DM, someone on shift if available, to help with the situation. The second DM should not be in front of the offender, either, as that will make it appear as if the DM's are

looking for a fight. The second DM should stand behind, and off to the side, of the person being talked to. That DM should also be standing at an angle to the person being talked to. If a third DM is available, that person would be on the opposite side, behind, in the same position as DM #2. Any more than that would be overkill, and look as if the DM's were looking for a fight. If more DM's are available, the best thing that they could do at that point is traffic control. Statistics have shown that most times, when a potential offender sees three DM's around him in strategic positions, he will back off. However, the occasional folly will happen. Because of these occasional follies, and the importance of ongoing DM training, the following procedures come from a class I attended in April 2002, and deal with different situations and different numbers of DM's available. In a one on one situation, the easiest way to defuse a situation is to ask the offender if he would like to talk in a more private setting, rather than make a scene and interrupt other players. By doing this, it has the appearance of giving the offender the upper hand, leaving the next move up to him. When in reality, the "more private place" you were talking about would be outside the party area and the play space, where you can more easily tell him to go home, and not let him back in. If the person resists or becomes confrontational, the safest thing to do, if you are a lone DM, would be to back up at 45-degree angles away from the offender and continue doing this each time the offender wants to become physical. This step back and away does three things. First it makes it harder for you, as a DM, to be hit. Second, it forces the person to have to move his entire body and shift his weight before he can strike out at you again, giving you time to consider alternatives, it gives the offender time to consider alternatives and it gives other DM's time to arrive. When a second DM is available, a good rule would be for the DM to come from the offender's line of sight and move to a position behind, and off to the side, of the person being talked to, remaining in the offender's peripheral vision. If a physical confrontation ensues at that point, DM2 can move in and "off balance" the offender. I do not recommend "take-downs". That is when DM2 knocks the offender off his or her feet or tackles them to the ground. The chances of injury and liability are greatly increased. The "off balance" maneuver is quick and easy and can be done by the smallest of DM's on the largest of offenders. DM2 moves quickly behind (for purposes of visualization, we will use the right side) behind and to the right of the offender. DM2 then places his left hand on the offender's left shoulder (from behind). With his left leg, DM2 presses his knee into the back of the offender's right knee, pressing down on the offender's left shoulder, to get the offender off balance. This does not take the offender to the ground, simply takes the initial fight out of the offender and puts him off balance. If a third DM is still unavailable, DM2 can hold the offender in that position while DM1 goes into the removal position, outlined below. Or DM2 can turn the offender by moving forward so that DM1 can then come from behind the offender to take the below outlined removal position. When someone needs to be removed physically, it requires only two DM's to accomplish this. By moving toward the offender's left arm from behind, DM1 can wrap his right arm under the offender's left arm and grab his wrist. Then the DM1 would place his left hand on the offender's left forearm or elbow. If DM2 can do the same thing in reverse on the opposite side, the offender can be moved out of the building regardless of his size or weight, just by pushing forward on his elbows. If a third DM is available, both DM2 and DM3 would be on opposite sides of the offender and at an angle behind him. If the offender becomes physical, both DM2 and DM3 could immediately go to the removal position and escort the offender out the door. Or if a third DM arrives while DM2 has the offender off balance, DM3 can immediately go to the removal position and DM2 can then take that same posture and remove the offender. If DM2 and DM3 have the offender in the removal position, DM1 simply needs to move out of the way and clear a path and open any doors so that DM2 and DM3 have a clear avenue to escort the offender out of the building. This should always be considered a last choice. Most situations do not need physical interference. The less intervention you do the more that people playing will enjoy themselves and the less hard feeling will be created. When in doubt, always err on the side of caution. And whenever possible, ask for a second opinion.

Basic First Aid:
The following safety module is intended to be used as refresher safety awareness reference and is in not intended to be used as a substitute for formal first aid training. This information was provided by the National Institute for Occupational Safety and Health, and has been modified to reflect the play party environment.

Get medical attention for all injuries:
It is very important for you to get immediate treatment for every injury, regardless how small you may think it is. Many cases have been reported where a small unimportant injury, such as a splinter wound or a puncture wound, quickly led to an infection. Even the smallest scratch is large enough for dangerous germs to enter, and in large bruises or deep cuts, germs come in by the millions. Immediate examination and treatment is necessary for every injury. The DM supervisor should have medical kits available for minor injuries.

What is first aid? It is simply those things you can do for the victim before medical help arrives. The most important procedures are described below.

Control bleeding with pressure:
Bleeding is the most visible result of an injury. Each of us has between five and six quarts of blood in our body. Most people can lose a small amount of blood with no problem, but if a quart or more is quickly lost, it could lead to shock and/or death. One of the best ways to treat bleeding is to place a clean cloth on the wound and apply pressure with the palm of your hand until the bleeding stops. You should also elevate the wound above the victim's heart, if possible, to slow down the bleeding at the wound site. Once the bleeding stops, do not try to remove the

cloth that is against the open wound as it could disturb the blood clotting and restart the bleeding. If the bleeding is very serious, apply pressure to the nearest major pressure point, located either on the inside of the upper arm between the shoulder and elbow, or in the groin area where the leg joins the body. Direct pressure is better than a pressure point or a tourniquet because direct pressure stops blood circulation only at the wound. Only use the pressure points if elevation and direct pressure haven't controlled the bleeding. Never use a tourniquet (a device, such as a bandage twisted tight with a stick, to control the flow of blood) except in response to an extreme emergency, such as a severed arm or leg. Tourniquets can damage nerves and blood vessels and can cause the victim to lose an arm or leg.

Treat physical shock quickly:
Shock can threaten the life of the victim of an injury if it is not treated quickly. Even if the injury doesn't directly cause death, the victim can go into shock and die. Shock occurs when the body's important functions are threatened by not getting enough blood or when the major organs and tissues don't receive enough oxygen. Some of the symptoms of shock are a pale or bluish skin color that is cold to the touch, vomiting, dull and sunken eyes, and unusual thirst. Shock requires medical treatment to be reversed, so all you can do is prevent it from getting worse. You can maintain an open airway for breathing, control any obvious bleeding and elevate the legs about 12 inches unless an injury makes it impossible. You can also prevent the loss of body heat by covering the victim (over and under) with blankets. Don't give the victim anything to eat or drink because this may cause vomiting. Generally, keep the victim lying flat on the back. A victim who is unconscious or bleeding from the mouth should lie on one side so breathing is easier. Stay with the victim until medical help arrives.

Move the injured person only when absolutely necessary:
Never move an injured person unless there is a fire or when explosives are involved. The major concern with moving an

injured person is making the injury worse, which is especially true with spinal cord injuries. If you must move an injured person, try to drag him or her by the clothing around the neck or shoulder area. If possible, drag the person onto a blanket or large cloth and then drag the blanket.

Perform the Heimlich maneuver on choking victims:
Ask the victim to cough, speak, or breathe. If the victim can do none of these things, stand behind the victim and locate the bottom rib with your hand. Move your hand across the abdomen to the area above the navel then make a fist and place your thumb side on the stomach. Place your other hand over your fist and press into the victim's stomach with a quick upward thrust until the food is dislodged.

Flush burns immediately with water:
There are a many different types of burns. They can be thermal burns, chemical burns, electrical burns or contact burns. Each of the burns can occur in a different way, but treatment for them is very similar. For thermal, chemical or contact burns, the first step is to run cold water over the burn for a minimum of 30 minutes. If the burn is small enough, keep it completely under water. Flushing the burn takes priority over calling for help. Flush the burn FIRST. If the victim's clothing is stuck to the burn, don't try to remove it. Remove clothing that is not stuck to the burn by cutting or tearing it. Cover the burn with a clean, cotton material. If you do not have clean, cotton material, do not cover the burn with anything. Do not scrub the burn and do not apply any soap, ointment, or home remedies. Also, don't offer the burn victim anything to drink or eat, but keep the victim covered with a blanket to maintain a normal body temperature until medical help arrives. If the victim has received an electrical burn, the treatment is a little different. Don't touch a victim who has been in contact with electricity unless you are clear of the power source. If the victim is still in contact with the power source, electricity will travel through the victim's body and electrify you when you reach to touch. Once the victim is clear of the power

source, your priority is to check for any airway obstruction, and to check breathing and circulation. Administer CPR if necessary. Once the victim is stable, begin to run cold water over the burns for a minimum of 30 minutes. Don't move the victim and don't scrub the burns or apply any soap, ointment, or home remedies. After flushing the burn, apply a clean, cotton cloth to the burn. If cotton is not available, don't use anything. Keep the victim warm and still and try to maintain a normal body temperature until medical help arrives.

Use cool treatment for heat exhaustion or stroke:
Heat exhaustion and heat stroke are two different things, although they are commonly confused as the same condition. Heat exhaustion can occur anywhere there is poor air circulation, or even if the person is poorly adjusted to very warm temperatures. The body reacts by increasing the heart rate and strengthening blood circulation. Simple heat exhaustion can occur due to loss of body fluids and salts. The symptoms are usually excessive fatigue, dizziness and disorientation, normal skin temperature but a damp and clammy feeling. To treat heat exhaustion, move to the victim to a cool spot and encourage drinking of cool water and rest. Heat stroke is much more serious and occurs when the body's sweat glands have shut down. Some symptoms of heat stroke are mental confusion, collapse, unconsciousness, fever with dry, mottled skin. A heat stroke victim will die quickly, so don't wait for medical help to arrive-- assist immediately. The first thing you can do is move the victim to a cool place out of the sun and begin pouring cool water over the victim. Fan the victim to provide good air circulation until medical help arrives.

Respond appropriately to the form of poisoning:
The first thing to do is get the victim away from the poison. Then provide treatment appropriate to the form of the poisoning. If the poison is in solid form, such as pills, remove it from the victim's mouth using a clean cloth wrapped around your finger. If the poison is a gas, remove the victim from the area and take to

fresh air. If the poison is corrosive to the skin, remove the clothing from the affected area and flush with water for 30 minutes. Take the poison container or label with you when you call for medical help because you will need to be able to answer questions about the poison. Try to stay calm and follow the instructions you are given. If the poison is in contact with the eyes, flush the victim's eyes for a minimum of 15 minutes with clean water.

Keep a first aid checklist:
In order to administer effective first aid, it is important to maintain adequate supplies in each first aid kit. First aid kits can be purchased commercially already stocked with the necessary supplies, or one can be made by including the following items: Adhesive bandages: available in a large range of sizes for minor cuts, abrasions and puncture wounds Butterfly closures: these hold wound edges firmly together. Rolled gauze: these allow freedom of movement and are recommended for securing the dressing and/or pads. These are especially good for hard-to-bandage wounds. Nonstick Sterile Pads: these are soft, super absorbent pads that provide a good environment for wound healing. These are recommended for bleeding and draining wounds, burns, and infections. First Aid Tapes: Various types of tapes should be included in each kit. These include adhesive, which is waterproof and extra strong for times when rigid strapping is needed; clear, which stretches with the body's movement, good for visible wounds; cloth, recommended for most first aid taping needs, including taping heavy dressings (less irritating than adhesive); and paper, which is recommended for sensitive skin and is used for light and frequently changed dressings. Items that also can be included in each kit are tweezers, first aid cream, thermometer, an analgesic or equivalent, and an ice pack. For more information about first aid kits, see the above section entitled "First Aid Kits", provided by the Federal Emergency Management Agency.

Report all injuries to the DM Supervisor:
As with getting medical attention for all injuries, it is equally important that you report all injuries to the DM supervisor. It is critical that the DM supervisor check into the causes of every party-related injury, regardless how minor, to find out exactly how it happened. There may be unsafe procedures or unsafe equipment that should be corrected.

Fill out an incident report:
Whenever an accident or incident occurs, it is safe to assume that some victims will want to blame someone else. At the very least, having an incident report sheet handy, to be filled out whenever an incident occurs, will go a long way to protect yourself and the organizers from any liability and can be used as a training tool, as well as to show areas that need to be monitored or corrected.

Fire Extinguishers:
We often hear people say, "If you're going to do 'fire play' keep a fire extinguisher nearby". But what do we know about fire extinguishers and what do we need to know about them? Portable fire extinguishers are classified to indicate their ability to handle specific classes and sizes of fires. Labels on extinguishers indicate the class and relative size of fire that they can be expected to handle. Class A extinguishers are used on fires involving ordinary combustibles, such as wood, cloth, and paper. Class B extinguishers are used on fires involving liquids, greases, and gases. Class C extinguishers are used on fires involving energized electrical equipment. Class D extinguishers are used on fires involving metals such as magnesium, titanium, zirconium, sodium, and potassium. The numerical value on the label tells you how big a fire or how big an area of fire the fire extinguisher can be expected to handle. A class 4-A extinguisher can be expected to handle twice as much as a class 2-A extinguisher. The way to use a fire extinguisher is broken down into this acronym: PASS. Pull, Aim, Squeeze, Sweep. Pull: Pull the pin out of the handle. Aim: Aim the nozzle at the fire. Squeeze: Squeeze the

trigger or handle. Sweep: Use a slow and steady, side to side motion to extinguish the fire.

The End of Your Shift:
Meet with your replacement and brief him or her on the current situation and any special circumstances. Answer any questions that they may have. Hand over equipment. Check out with the DM Supervisor.

Various Groups Social Rules:
SAADE Party & Social Rules SAADE recognizes that Scene Etiquette is dynamic and personal. It differs depending on the individual and the situation. SAADE hereby adopts and promotes the practice of Scene Etiquette, which fosters courtesy and respect among individuals within the leather community. We would ask our members and their guests to follow these rules while attending SAADE meetings, functions and/or any SAADE special interest group.

Social Rules:
It is inappropriate to touch other people's person or property without first obtaining permission. Never assume. Communication is the key to initiating play or determining the level of intimacy you may have toward another. The basic premise is consent. Be sure you have consent before you move ahead to play or touch. Do NOT join a scene unless specifically asked to do so! Play scenes are personal and the area in which they take place is to be respected. Again consent is the issue. Do not assume you are a welcome addition to any scene that is being undertaken unless you are specifically asked to join in. We ask all SAADE members to practice situational awareness. Be aware! Sometimes we invade or disrupt play scenes unintentionally. Keep conversation, laughter and/or comments to a minimum in the play areas. Don't make any loud noises or disruptions that may break the play space. We ask that you check the proximity of yourself to the play areas and be respectful of the events that are unfolding. We understand that conflict

happens in life. Sometimes misunderstandings occur and bad feeling result from them. We ask that members strive to resolve these conflicts outside of the SAADE events. Feel free to discuss problems with the SAADE council but know that we recommend that members try to get together, one on one, to discuss their issues and work them out between themselves. If this is not possible we ask that you avail yourselves to the D/s Mediation team or get a trusted 3rd party to help resolve your differences. Please remember, as a whole, we are not a political group. SAADE's mission is fun, education and community building. There are other venues for political wrangling. This is a neutral zone for exploring the things we have in common. Being mindful that Scene Etiquette is expected of all SAADE members. Willful and ongoing disrespect of other members may be grounds for the suspension of membership privileges and/or terminating membership and the attendance to SAADE functions and special interest groups.

Party Rules:
All attendees must present their membership card for admission, or be a guest of a card-carrying member. Guests are the sole responsibility of the sponsoring member. They are expected to know the rules and be accepting of our lifestyle and play. The member will be held responsible for the guest's behavior. Each member may bring up to two guests. Prostitution, solicitation, and negotiation of compensation for sexual services ARE ILLEGAL and are not tolerated. Violations shall result in immediate removal and banning from future events. Scene professionals may not accept payment for any services rendered at a SAADE event. All play shall be Consensual. Normal scene etiquette is required. Do not monopolize the equipment (A good rule of thumb if people are waiting for equipment is not to stay on any one piece of equipment for more than 70 minutes). Attendees must be over eighteen years of age. Bring your own equipment, props and toys for your type of play. Treat the hosts' home with respect. Please clean up after your scene. Leave all equipment free of sweat, blood, other bodily fluids, wax, toys, etc. Bring

bodily fluid concerns to the attention of the DMs. Wax, fire, water sports and scenes involving bodily fluids need to be brought to the DM's attention prior to play. If an area has been set aside for those purposes, only use the area set aside for those purposes. Place the fire extinguisher next to the scene, and have a wet towel next to you, a bowl of water and whatever other safety precautions need to be in place. Also, arrange for a "second". Smoke in designated areas only. And please use the ashtrays provided. (DM's will know where these areas are). No illegal substances of any kind are allowed at SAADE events. Firearms and firearm replicas may not be brought into any SAADE event. Safe sex is recommended, if you choose to do this type of scene. Do not touch other people's person or property without first asking permission. Never assume a sub is "fair game". No one is fair game here. Always ask first. Never handle other people's toys or toy bag without permission. Help clean up after the party.

Dungeon Monitor's Role:
All SAADE sponsored play parties will have at least one Dungeon Monitor (DM) per fifty (50) attendees. The DM shall not be encumbered with any other duties that may distract him/her from the role of DM. The DM will have access to all areas during an event. Do not interrupt a scene. If you have a concern, bring it to the attention of a DM. Only DMs may interrupt scenes. The SAADE council has faith in their DMs, so decisions made by the DM concerning safety, security or removal is final. Additional House Rules may also apply, depending upon location, host, and/or other circumstances.

SSCN Social Rules:
Etiquette Statement:
SSCN recognizes that Scene Etiquette is dynamic and personal. It differs depending on the individual and the situation. SSCN hereby adopts and promotes the practice of Scene Etiquette, which fosters courtesy and respect among individuals within the leather community. Being mindful of "Scene Etiquette" is

strongly encouraged. Willful and ongoing disrespect of other Contributors may be grounds for expulsion. (Section 4.05) Social Rules (These apply to ALL SSCN sponsored events) All play shall be Consensual. All SSCN sponsored play socials must have at least one Dungeon Monitor (DM), appointed by the Board, on duty at all times. The DM shall not be encumbered with any other duties that may distract him/her from the role of DM. The DM will have access to all areas during an event. All concerns should be brought to the attention of the DM. Only DMs may interrupt a scene. The decisions made by the DM are final. No illegal substances of any kind are allowed on the premises. Firearms and firearm replicas may not be brought into any SSCN event. All attendees must present their Contributor card for admission, or be a guest of a card-carrying Contributor. Upon entry, all guests shall read, sign and agree to abide by the SSCN rules for socials and in addition present a valid photo ID to verify their identity. Prostitution, solicitation, and negotiation of compensation for sexual services ARE ILLEGAL and are not tolerated. Violations shall result in immediate removal and banning from future events. Scene professionals may not accept payment, at a SSCN event, for any services rendered. Normal scene etiquette is required (i.e., Do not interfere with a scene, do not invade scene space, etc). Please keep conversation, laughter and comments to a minimum in the play area. Do not monopolize the equipment. Do NOT join a scene unless specifically asked to do so! Please clean up after your scene. Leave all equipment free of sweat, blood, other bodily fluids, wax, toys, etc. Bring bodily fluid concerns to the attention of the DM. Wax, fire, and scenes involving bodily fluids need prior permission of the DM, unless a designated area has been set aside for those purposes. Cameras and other types of recording devices are NOT allowed at any SSCN sponsored event without the expressed written permission of the Board of Directors, and prior notice to attendees. Additional House Rules may also apply, depending upon location, host, and/or other circumstances.

Society of Janus Party Rules and Play Space Protocol:
No food or drink (except water in non-breakable containers) is
allowed in the play areas. No illegal activities - Do not engage in
any illegal activities on the premises. No alcohol, illegal drugs,
inhalants or other intoxicants are allowed unless prescribed by a
doctor. Fragrances or heavy scents of any kind e.g. perfume,
cologne, incense, etc. are strongly discouraged.

Guests:
You are only allowed to invite four guests to a party. Your guests
are your responsibility at all times. They must arrive with, or after
you, and leave with, or before you. No exceptions. Please watch
respectfully and quietly - Do not participate in loud talk or idle
chatter in the play area. Do not sit on the play equipment or in
the playing spaces, unless you are playing. There are chairs,
benches and the floor available for that purpose.

Hands Off:
Never touch someone else or their toys, props or other property,
without asking and receiving permission. Unusually loud or
otherwise disruptive play - Inform the Dungeon Monitor or the
event's director before beginning any loud, messy or disruptive
play that may affect the players around you.

Wax and/or fire play:
Because of the unusually messy or dangerous nature of this type
of play, please obtain permission from a Dungeon Monitor
before you start your scene. Voyeurism is welcome as long as it is
discreet and does not disturb the players; if in doubt, move back.
Remember, the primary purpose of this scene is play. Spectators
must always give way to players, even if it means leaving a room.

Experience:
The players in the scene vary widely in experience and styles of
play, so don't be quick to judge the play of others based on your
own. On the other hand, if you observe play in which safety or

health rules are being ignored; please inform a Dungeon Monitor or the Event Director immediately.

Safewords:
We recommend the use of safewords when playing together. In emergency situations where outside assistance is required, our scene safeword is "SAFEWORD". "SAFEWORD" is our version of 911. Do not abuse or misuse this word!

Be Clean:
Protect the play surfaces during your play. CLEAN UP the area thoroughly afterwards.

Leaving the premises:
You may not return without notifying the Door Monitor in advance.

No exchange of body fluids is permitted:
All body fluids must be contained within your play area and may not be introduced into the body of another, or upon broken skin. You must not allow any blood or semen to fly from tips of canes, whips, or other implements. Barrier protection is mandatory when fucking, fingering, fisting, or having oral/genital sex with anyone - male or female. Masturbators also must wear a condom. Safe sex supplies have been provided for your use.

Blood Play (including temporary piercings):
Instruments that have drawn blood should be disposed of, put away, or cleaned immediately before being used again. Anything bloodied during play must be cleaned and isolated to avoid contact with others. Sharps containers are available for disposal of contaminated needles. Permission must be obtained from the Dungeon Monitor prior to starting any blood play. No scat or water sports will be allowed.

Naked people:
Must sit on sheets or towels (bring your own) when sitting on absorbent surfaces.

House Rules:
Depending on the location of the event, special "house rules" may apply.

If your group would like to have Me give them this course, email me at sirbamm@sirbamm.com

Eight Levels of Domination

Most of the information below was gathered from other web sites. It's been revised a few times. The original text was found at Geocities/esubmissive. I am sorry that I do not know who the original author was. This is another source of information to help you figure out where you are, establish what you want, help you get what you need and direct you to where you want to go within the leather-BDSM-fetish scene. It is not meant to be a rule book, but rather a guide, and is not meant to be taken as legal, medical or religious advice. I will use the male form for the Top and the female for the bottom, only for purposes of ease in writing.

1 The non-dominant (or kinky person):
He is not into a power exchange or being in control. He only enjoys the heightened sexuality that the D/s scene brings to him. He feels "safe" in the scene if both he and his partner are having fun. He normally won't try new things without first being told by the submissive what specific things she would enjoy. His pleasure is from the sexual activity and not from S/M or being in control.

2 The role playing Dominant:
This person is normally found on-line. He will act "Dom-ly" and appear to be in control. He may be into humiliation and enjoy role playing. He will have the submissive cyber-serve him, kneel, and will act the role, just as he wants the submissive to act her role. He likes to "train" new submissives because he feels safe when his charge has little knowledge about D/s. The Dominant will normally not "force" the submissive to do things or request things that will push the submissive's limits. The only time he may push is to have cybersex. This type of "Dominant" will usually brag about the slaves he has had and the slaves that he has trained.

3 The Top:
This person likes to play "Master" and likes to feel in control. He will want to have his submissive wear his collar before they have

established a relationship. He may have the submissive serve him and his needs. He, likely, doesn't concentrate on the relationship or the submissive's growth, only on the upcoming scene. He seldom gives the submissive exercises, and if he does, he will normally give very little feedback when the assignment is turned in. He will be in control most of the time, but not use the control for mutual growth or benefit.

4 The Dominant non-Master:
This type of person controls the submissive, but it is usually temporary and within agreed upon limits. The big difference between this person and the ones mentioned above is that this one knows that he needs the submissive in order to have the power. He is usually turned on by being served, receiving sexual gratification, in scene and outside of scenes. They do not gain satisfaction from forcing the submissive to submit to their way. They usually dictate the scene based on the agreed limits. Even though they seek their pleasure from being in control, the submissive will find it easy to top from the bottom.

5 The Dominant, play Master:
This type of person also takes control but it is usually temporary and within agreed limits. He gains satisfaction from being served and serviced. Normally he controls the scene and is into bondage and light pain. He may use a spanking device to the point of pain, but does not go far enough to build up endorphins in the submissive. If there is pain in the scene, he may, indirectly, derive pleasure from being in control and causing the pain, but not because of the feelings the submissive may have. This person controls the submissive, but not the scene. The scene will usually end at the same level of intensity at which it started.

6 The True Dominant:
This person dominates the relationship but may have agreed upon limits. The true Dominant wants to be served by the submissive. He enjoys this in both erotic and non-erotic services by having the submissive take care of his wants and needs within

their agreed upon terms. This person will only take the dominant role when he is in the mood. Many times he will play the role for days at a time, but he retains his prerogative to quit at any time. The time period is usually agreed to in advance or falls within the time constraints that they have together. You may find this person in short or long term relationships with his submissive. He normally has good reasons why he can't enter a full time relationship and he controls when he will be Dominant. This type of person will usually give the submissive assignments, but may not question her if they are not completed and may not give feedback even if they are.

7 The part-time Master:
The part time Master will have an on-going relationship as Master/slave and he thinks of his slave as his property at all times. He wants the slave to grow and he tries to distinguish between the slave's wants and needs. The part time Master will usually rule the submissive's life to the point that he will give her assignments, tell her how to act and may tell her what to wear. He devotes only his free time to the slave. This type of person will use scenes to help the slave to grow, as well. He usually knows how to control the pain experience and push the slave's limits. He watches the changes the slave makes during scenes and helps her grow outside of scenes. The part-time Master will also help the slave reach subspace. The part-time Master will perform aftercare after the scene to take care of the slave's needs.

8 The 24/7 Master:
This person takes control of the relationship and thinks of the slave's well-being. Limits in the relationship are considered opportunities for growth and the slave has duties and obligations to perform. He regards the slave as a possession and spends his time grooming the slave. His day to day role is very similar to the "vanilla" husband, except that his role is stricter, because he is the keeper of the relationship and in charge of her well-being as a slave. Because of the total power exchange in which he accepts power over the slave's life, (physical, emotional, and mental), this

kind of arrangement is usually entered into much more carefully than a traditional marriage. Normally, contracts are signed specifying what the slave's role will be and what time period it will cover. The contract is normally based on rules of D/s, S/M etiquette; their agreed upon limits, prior negotiations and it will establish areas for growth. The contract may include clauses about who may break the contract, for what reasons and what needs to be done in order to break the contract, and whether or not it is renewable.

Edge Play

A friend of Mine, pix, in the southeastern Ohio area, wrote a great post on one of the lists that I belong to on the topic of edge play. With her permission, I have used a lot of her information below. Oour views on edge play differ slightly. However, it was so thought provoking that I decided to dedicate a few pages to this topic.

The entire article was originally posted on SE Ohio BDSM, under "Edgeplay". All of the articles from there and in the Founder's Forum were to be put into a manuscript; I don't know what came of that. Numerous attempts have been made in an attempt to find out.

Those Who Know, Do
A lot of BDSMers in pix's area say that they are edge players. And they will say what there type of play is, but, they won't say much more about it. she says that their credo is, "We don't speak our kink in details."

pix goes on to say that this happens for a few reasons. First, edge players are still one of the few groups shunned by the alternative lifestyle community. On the scale of "kinkable distaste" they say that they are often made to feel like they fall somewhere slightly above snuff, bestiality & pedophilia. The less they talk with the community at large, the less they are ostracized and excluded.

Second, edge players feel they hold a responsibility to "keep it away from the newbies" so that people entering the lifestyle aren't scared off by such extremes or so that people interested don't try dangerous activities without first knowing the basic safety of BDSM.

Lastly, edge players very much tire of the stereotypes that alternative lifestylists have about them, and they want to spend their time having fun instead of educating & fighting stereotypes the way they would outside of the community.

I guess I've been lucky. In the areas that I've lived in there have been a lot more people doing edge-type play, so I always felt more like the "norm" than the "outcast". And like pix, My interests have always been in the fields of how the law effects What It Is That We Do and educating the SM community, as well as the vanilla community. My various commitments in the past to the National Coalition for Sexual Freedom (NCSF) as a Coalition Partner Board Member and Second Tier Incident Responder, as the GWNN liaison to the NCSF, as a contributor to the SAADE Guide on Dealing with Law Enforcement at Your Door, as a Mentor with the SAADE Mentor Group, along with the various presentations and demonstrations I've done – and still do - further that goal and that ideal.

What is edge play?
Is it edge play to the players involved, or only to those watching? According to *steel-door*, edge play is: "... the action of offering new challenges to the Edges of play you and your submissive are already familiar with." Both pix and I usually hear people refer to "Edge Play" as anything inherently dangerous, such as knife play, electrical play, breath control, blood sports, fire play, needle play, etc.

Tonight, I went to a party where there were only edge players. And this very topic came up. Is it really SSC that Wwe're doing or is it really risk aware consensual kink? And how much of what Wwe do is really edge play? And is it edgy to the others in Oour group or just to outsiders? One slave made the analogy that she thinks that anyone who jumps out of an airplane is insane and that behavior isn't safe to her, but to the people doing it, it's absolutely perfect.

For most of Uus, both of the definitions in this section are correct. For some, dangerous play is called edge play because for most people that is the edge of where the players have gone. For others, edge play is a bit more difficult to explain. And it isn't based on the people watching, because most edge play takes place without anyone watching. There aren't DM's or "seconds", and the focus is so intent on what You are doing that You wouldn't notice if people were watching anyway; besides for the fact that most of the really edgy play is not permitted at most public parties.

There is danger in most types of BDSM play. Even a simple hand spanking, done incorrectly, can lead to permanent damage. Is knife intimidation play really edge play? Are temporary needle piercings really considered edgy?

Is breath play the only play that is truly edge play? Because in breath play there is no way of signaling a safeword before it's too late and it also may be the only type of play in which there are no signs of trouble. A bottom doesn't know when they are going to pass out because they feel extremely relaxed. Even if they could identify this euphoria as a precursor to passing out, by the time they reach this point, they have lost too much oxygen to the brain to articulate the need for air and they have less than a fraction of a second before they are unconscious.

What may really separate edge play from typical play isn't so much the danger involved, but the lack of recourse if that danger line is crossed. Just like we practice "safer" sex rather than "safe" sex, so might Oour definitions of SSC be manipulated. Wwe play "safer", "saner" and consensual rather than "safe", "sane" and consensual. And this is where pix and I disagree. she feels that edge players rarely adhere to the credo of Safe, Sane & Consensual themselves (although, she says, most feel it is a good policy, encourage it highly, introduce newcomers to SSC, but it just isn't for them, in their play). I feel that each person's interpretation of SSC dictates what is and is not safe, based upon their knowledge, skill level and the length of time with their partner.

So, What's Up With That?

Many edge players aren't sure, themselves, why they do it. Some say the endorphins from fear are a factor. Some thrive on the danger. Some have a fascination with the realm of death they can't experience through typical play. A few even admit that they have issues and edge play is a way of escaping those issues. Some do it for the total and complete surrender of their very life to their partner. Some do it because it has become an obsession or a fetish. Some do it because it takes them to a whole new subspace. Some do it because they are extreme emotional or physical masochists. There are probably as many reasons for edge play as there are for typical play.

Most edge players specialize in a specific area of edge play. Most are highly educated in their particular interest and they restrict their edge play to a limited number of partners who are also educated in that area. Most are strongly against mind-altering substances. And most edge playing bottoms are also attention sluts.

In Closing

It is the general opinion that betrayal of Safe, Sane and Consensual is reason enough to exclude someone from a group or party; and edge players don't want to be excluded. They also don't want to scare people away. And by all means, they don't want others to engage in the things that they do without knowing what they are doing.

Some edge players also take a lot of ridicule or insult for their style of play. I can't tell you how many times have people come up to My! t and told her that she was crazy; or that what she is doing is sick.

All I can say is "Keep educating and keep learning."

Scene Etiquette

Bits and pieces of information on scene etiquette were spread throughout My site, SirBamm.com; however, it is such an important topic, and one that keeps coming up so often, that I decided to dedicate an article in this book to the subject.

Play Party Etiquette:
The following contains information about BDSM play party etiquette. It was originally written for users of the Usenet newsgroup *alt.sex.bondage,* and was intended to cover both events held in public spaces and events held in private homes. I have adapted where appropriate and changed things where I felt I needed to; and although not every suggestion is relevant to every situation, the basic ideas are universal.

The goal of the following paragraphs is to describe play party customs and etiquette that often are not stated in the rules. The original text was found at: *sexuality.org/Play_Party_Etiquette.* Etiquette and protocol differ slightly in different regions, and within the same area, in different circles. However, some pretty uniform rules are basic to all of them.

Do not touch people, even in what you think of as a friendly way (like touching someone's arm in conversation) without asking permission. In most BDSM circles, hugging someone in even a casual way without the prior verbal assurance that it is welcome is considered overstepping boundaries. Just because someone may be standing naked next to you does not make it ok to stroke that person's ass - in fact, it is not ok to stroke even the person's arm! And it surely isn't ok to spank or paddle their ass when they walk by. The working assumption is that touch of any kind is not ok without asking. On the other hand, asking to hug or shake hands or look at the piercing someone is flaunting is certainly acceptable and not considered an offense in any way, just so long as the asker does not act offended if the answer is not what he wanted to hear.

Leave space for the top to move, swing a flogger, etc. during a scene. If the room is too crowded, stand against the far wall or leave the room. If the top asks you to move, then move.

Be quiet while scenes are going on, or go to the social area to chat. Be polite, and don't talk or whisper. Yours could be the remark that ruins a wonderful scene for someone or disturbs their sub space or Dom Space.

A novice attempting to start conversations with the top or the bottom during scenes is one of the most common and astonishing etiquette errors at play parties with new people in attendance. Do not address comments or questions to the top or the bottom while they are playing. Similarly, do not try to start a conversation with the partners while they are cuddling together after a scene. What looks to you like a lull in the action while the top steps away to get a new toy or while the partners are whispering intimately together after a scene is not the moment to walk over and ask questions or make comments. The partners are very focused on each other and on the intimacy of whatever they are doing together, and they want to maintain that focus even during breaks. If you feel an uncontrollable urge to ask how the top ever learned to wield a knife so steadily, or to ask if the bottom isn't scared of having a nipple cut off, then go get a soda and ask someone in the social area.

Do not ever touch or get too close to the bottom during or after a scene. Bottoms are dependent on their tops; the bottom's physical and emotional well-being is the top's responsibility during and after scenes. After a scene, give the players a quiet space on the sofa if they want to cuddle together. The closeness and aftercare following scenes and the bottom's emotional fragility usually last longer than it looks to outsiders. Give people time to come down. If you need to ask a quiet question, like "Would you like a blanket?" or "Would you like a glass of water?"

address the top, not the bottom, and be as unobtrusive, succinct, and quiet as possible.

Do not join in scenes, even if it looks like they are free-for-alls. A scene that might look to you like lots of folks are joining in to pleasure or otherwise play with the bottom might in fact be pre-arranged between the top and other acceptable players to look casual. Or it might be that the top is subtly signaling audience members he knows to be acceptable. Join in only if the top clearly beckons you in. If in doubt, err on the side of caution. In other words, don't - or check with the top.

Do not come on to people in a clueless manner. Hounding, harassing, or puppy-dogging after the object of your sexual interest will guarantee that you will not be invited to any more parties; you might even be thrown out of the one you are at.

Most people like to be complimented on their scenes. If you like a particular top or bottom, telling them what you liked about their scene is usually well-received. But wait until they are walking about and socializing again. Asking interesting how-to questions is also a good way to make friends. But again, wait until later.

Do not intervene in scenes. If you are bothered by something you see because it seems extreme, risky, or even impossible to be consensual to you, find a host or DM to check on the scene, explain it to you, or reassure you. If a corrective action like a safety improvement needs to be taken, the host or DM will take care of conveying that to the top in an appropriate manner. When you are more experienced you will be able to recognize if something is possibly nonconsensual or unduly dangerous. At your first few play parties, plan to absorb and watch and learn. If something is too extreme for you to enjoy watching, then simply leave the room - quietly.

Do not touch people's toys, floggers, etc. that are lying around without finding the owner and asking. Even if someone lets you hold a flogger, it is also courteous to ask again before swinging it through the air at an imaginary target or your forearm. Do not run a knife or Wartenberg pinwheel along your skin to test its sharpness - the owner might have gone to pains to sterilize the blade in expectation of an upcoming scene, and sharp edges break skin without always leaving marks or drawing blood.

Clean up play furniture or play areas when you are done using them. Pick up your toys so someone else can use the play area without stumbling on your belongings. Wipe down the play furniture so it is not sweaty for the next person, and if any bodily fluids were spilled accidentally, clean them up thoroughly - hosts often provide appropriate cleaning materials if you don't have them on hand.

Do not hog play furniture for hours on end with your scene. If you are unsure, ask the host for an estimate of a reasonable amount of time to use the play furniture or equipment.

At the party, relax, be yourself, be open and friendly; ask questions if you need to make conversation; listen to what others have to say. Bring your sense of humor.

Bring munchies if the hosts suggested it. Quality breads, homemade desserts, and fresh fruit are desirable food items in many play circles, are more welcome and more likely to be devoured and complimented than a bag of chips. In many play circles, alcohol and other drugs are forbidden at play parties; do not bring these without checking with the host.

Help clean up before you leave! Don't offer and then wait for instructions - just do it. Those ten used plastic cups you gather up and toss out, or the empty dip dish you wash and leave in the drainer to dry at 3 a.m., or the ice bucket you refill mid-party just because you noticed it was empty will save the host a lot of work and mean more invitations to parties in the future.

Do not mention anyone at the party to those not at the party without that person's express permission. Especially, do not post to any public forum in a way that identifies someone else without permission. Even mentioning someone in email without that person's permission can be considered a violation of etiquette. Outing someone because you thought it was way cool to describe some hot scene you got to see, or for any other reason, is Not Ok. It is usually ok to describe people's scenes in a manner that leaves the participants - and the hosts - unidentifiable, but even then it is customary to ask first. It is also customary to email copies of anything you post in a public forum to all people referenced or described therein, in advance, if there is anything you are in doubt about, or whether the party is mentionable or not. The rule of thumb is that parties are not mentionable publicly unless stated otherwise.

Clothes and gender usually don't tell you anything about a person's interests, predilections, or experience levels. Unless the party rules specify that fetish wear is required, people generally dress however they like to dress. Some people use clothes and flags to signal their interests, but in practice the majority of experienced players do not unless clothing styles are separate pleasures for them. Some deeply devoted and owned submissives do not wear collars and do not hover at the feet of their owners at parties. Clothing can be a separate fetish.

Don't gape at scenes, behavior, or sexual proclivities that are new for you to actually encounter in real life even if you've heard of such things and wished for years you could actually see it. There is a fine line between open-minded curiosity - the desire to learn and understand something that is new for you from those who indicate (in the social area) that they are willing to take the time to share and converse with you about their play styles and sexual interests - versus prurient judgmentalism, gawking, or tiresomely asking someone who is sick of being asked what he or she can possibly enjoy by doing whatever astonishing thing you saw the person do. Be sensitive about when and who you ask, and be sensitive while you watch. People at play parties are not there to entertain or educate you, even though many folks who choose to attend play parties do also enjoy the exhibitionist and educational aspects of what they are doing. Be sensitive to what each individual is offering to strangers, and don't rudely assume they are offering you a private show, lesson, educational experience, or opportunity to giggle like a school child at some porn you have amazingly gotten lucky enough to see outside of a magazine.

Be tolerant of things you didn't expect. In particular, even if you are fascinated, try not to gawk noticeably at stuff you personally have never encountered before. Watching and learning are fine - and are often exactly the point - but there is a social norm in each group about what is appropriate astonishment to show to those around you. If you have never seen two males play sexually and lovingly together before, or if you find watching the two women playing together across the room really hot for you as a voyeur, or if you have never talked to a cross-dresser close enough to actually hold a social conversation while you are standing around getting soda in the social area, get a grip on yourself before you start behaving like a ten-year-old telling a joke with a naughty word in it! If you never expected and are shocked by the amount of blood from a ritual cutting, or by what appears to you to be the hate-filled screaming and cursing of a bottom raging at her top at the height of a difficult scene, or if you never envisioned seeing a piercing of a needle right through someone's nipple, or if whatever else you didn't expect and are suddenly encountering seems extreme to you, then the astonishment is probably yours.

In advance of the party, read a few books on BDSM and try to pick up a few pointers about what you might see. There is plenty of wonderful information on various pages throughout this web site and links to other equally wonderful sites. You might even pick up some fine points of etiquette, like how to behave toward submissives that aren't yours. Hint: A submissive is only submissive to the people that she chooses to submit to. If she doesn't belong to you, do not expect her to treat you as such.

No one, who is not your own personal partner, owes any deference to you beyond common, everyday courtesy. No one is required to fetch you a drink or defer to your opinion in conversation.

Details of D/s etiquette are tricky and there are some uncommon etiquette delicacies. Err on the side of caution in all things leather/SM/fetish related.

You can and should talk to the host during the party or, if more appropriate, afterwards to ask unanswered questions, say thank you, and follow up in any ways you like. If you felt uncomfortable about anything at all at the party, talking to the host afterwards is an excellent idea. Hosts usually want to help their guests learn and sort themselves out according to comfort levels. Hosts, usually, also want feedback so they can create environments that accommodate a variety of comfort levels and so they can decide what kinds of play and which attendees make for enjoyable parties. And if the host ran out of the kind of soda everyone was standing in the social area dying for, the host wants to know. If a host never hears about the individual you felt harassed by in the social area or while you were playing, or that you felt some kind of play you watched was unnecessarily dangerous and you had no DMs you could approach and didn't know the customs about how to handle the situation, the host cannot possibly make the necessary reforms. The host wants to know, and it is your responsibility as a responsible attendee to take the initiative to inform the host.

And it is your responsibility to thank the host. Follow up email is always welcome. And don't think for a moment that hosts do not notice those who take a moment to send a thank you, even if they already said thanks when they left the party.

Etiquette for Scene Onlookers:
Particular etiquette for watching a scene can vary from place to place. There may be completely different rules in a large city Pay for Play Dungeon & the privacy of one's home with a group of close friends. Old School, New School, East Coast, West Coast.... rules vary. This particular piece of writing focuses on smaller group gatherings and contains some of the guidelines you'll find most anywhere. The main thing to remember is that this time is for the people scening, not you. You wouldn't go jump up on the stage in the middle of a theater play, nor should you interrupt during a scene. You are the audience. They are the players. Let them play.

Look but don't touch!

It should be drilled in everyone's head thoroughly that you never touch the people engaging in a scene. Don't touch the Top. Don't touch the bottom. Unless you are specifically invited to do so by the Top, you should assume that those people are completely off limits to any type of touching, even a pat on the back or brushing against them if you need to walk past.

As well as not touching the people engaging in a scene, you should also make a point of not touching any of the equipment or toys that they are using or have laid out to use. You may occasionally see another Dominant hand the Top a toy. Chances are that these people know each other well. Don't take it upon yourself as a Dominant to stand there handing the Top cool items out of your toy-bag. Have a seat and show off your goodies later.

Don't change the lighting, fans, thermostat or music.

These are probably things that have been adjusted by the people scening before the scene starts. If it's too dark to see (as in a fear provoking scene), you don't have much of an option except listening. If it's too bright (as it can often be in an interrogation scene), simply shade your eyes. The fans and thermostat are probably set for the comfort of those scening. Usually the Top is working up a great sweat while the bottom is about to shiver. Let them choose how they are going to adjust the room's temperature depending on their needs. Absolutely don't touch the music. Don't change the choice of music or the music volume level. All of these elements are part of how those scening get into their headspace. Sometimes the Top may motion for someone to change the volume, fans, lights, etc... Then, and only then is it ok to do so. Just be sure that you are the one being addressed and you understand what adjustments you need to make.

Keep the noise level down.

If you are talking or commenting to the person next to you, keep it in a whisper, the same, if not more so than you would in a theater. The key is to be sure that those scening can't hear you. By all means do not laugh! The last thing a naked bottom hung from the ceiling needs to hear is people laughing. If you feel you must laugh, try to stifle it in a pillow. If you absolutely can't control yourself, leave the room. Don't bustle around trying to clean up the room or get people drinks. Do that before or after the scene, not during.

When a Top asks for audience participation, they NEED it.

If a Top is doing a humiliation scene, S/He may ask the audience to drill the submissive with embarrassing questions, bark, oink, shout insults, or whatever. Some scenes may require some very absurd sounding audience participation requests. S/He may want people to clap, whistle, throw things at the bottom, count aloud as lashes are delivered, etc.. S/He may ask each person in turn to name something they want to see done to the bottom, choose a number, letter, name a profession, crime or any other number of odd sounding requests.

The Top will generally be the one asking the audience to participate. If a Top asks the audience to do such things, try to make an effort to join in and be a good sport. The partners have probably either negotiated this ahead of time or they are a long-term couple. By not joining in, you deny the players that element of the scene. If you absolutely feel you can't participate, just say "I pass." so they can move on in a timely manner to the next audience member.

The subbie shuffle.

When/if the bottom hits subspace, don't be surprised to see everyone getting up and bustling around. The Dominants are most likely assisting the Top in getting the bottom's limp body down off the cross, out of suspension, etc... They will quickly re-take their seats once the submissive is down.

submissives on the other hand...

This can almost be an amusing sight.

When a submissive is lowered down from suspension, it is not at all unlikely to see 5 other submissives running around the room getting glasses of water, blankets, pillows, sodas, moving objects out of the way, and asking the Top if they need the lighting or temperature changed. Most of these submissives are not out of line at all by doing this. They probably either know the bottom well or know what s/he needs for aftercare, or they have been trained as service subs/slaves and they feel bound by duty to tend to either the Top or the bottom, or are Dungeon Monitors. You may see 3 submissives carrying one glass of water because they understand that all of them have a duty to do this. After they have performed the duties they were trained to do, they too will re-take their seats or leave the room.

Other submissives will not move from their seat at all after the scene. They have probably had the opposite training of not interrupting. It is not a bit rude for a submissive to remain in his/her seat silently continuing to watch the full aftercare of the bottom. They are fulfilling their obligation.

A note about safewords:
The universal safewords for a bottom to use are "green" (i'd like more, faster, harder, etc...) "yellow" (You need to slow down, ease back, give me a second to recuperate.) and "red" (All stop immediately!). As an onlooker, you should refrain from using these words in conversation during a scene, even in a whisper. If you hear a bottom use green or yellow, you should remain silent. Even if a bottom calls yellow and the Top does not slow down, do not interfere. That bottom still has the option of calling red and the Top may be pushing limits.

If you hear a bottom call "red" you should immediately turn all attention to the people scening. The red safety call is a call to EVERYONE in the room, not just the Top. We all hope and pray that if a bottom calls red, the Top will immediately stop, but if S/He doesn't for some reason, then we must face the sticky situation of intervening. This can be a very difficult thing to do, and some guidelines have been set on how to do this. Watch the Top to see if they are stopping. They may look like they are continuing the scene when in actuality they are removing clamps, caressing the skin, etc... If the Top is not stopping, do not immediately assume they are being abusive. They may be in a Top space and did not hear the red call. Get the attention of a DM, if one isn't already on scene. At this point, it may become appropriate for onlookers to say "s/he called red. You need to stop." or to address the bottom by saying "call again if you need to." Again, at this point we all hope and pray the Top stops. If not, the scene you are watching has turned from play to abuse. Immediately notify the host or DM.

You should only intervene if the slave loses consciousness (which is different from going limp from subspace) or if serious or permanent damage is inflicted. This probably won't happen because the Master/Mistress cares for the slave. Most sadists will watch this type of scene and close friends of the couple will probably watch. Many others will dismiss themselves from the room. That's ok. If you can't take watching this type of scene, quietly leave the room.

Aftercare:
After the scene has finished, the players may very well be situated in the middle of the room because that's where the bottom ended up. After they have engaged in some light aftercare, they will probably move to a sofa or other location. Until they move, consider the scene still in progress, but at this point it is usually ok to get up to get a drink, go outside for fresh air or a cigarette, etc... Don't touch any of the toys they were using. They still need to be cleaned. Don't take it upon yourself to clean the toys. Many times this is the bottom's responsibility or they are toys that the Top doesn't want others to handle.

The main thing to remember about being an audience member during a scene is to be quiet and polite. As an onlooker, you are there to watch, nothing more.

Etiquette for those who are new to the scene or fresh off the Internet:
Most people that have been around for any length of time say, "Well, it's common sense". But people that have all of their "real experience" as a Top in chat rooms or on the Internet don't seem to get this. The following is not a suggestion or an opinion. It is plain, simple, hard facts, and are not negotiable.

Being a "Real Time" Dominant is not the same as being a Cyber Dom!

The "experience" cyber-doms have is that they can talk to any sub on the internet and say, "On your knees, bitch, and suck my cock" and the person on the other end of the connection will tell them how much she enjoys what she's doing and tell them all about what she's doing and what a great Dominant they are and how she never felt as good in her life.

That's not how it works in the real world. Be polite, respectful and humble around anyone you do not know intimately, or you very well may be asked to leave, and possibly be told not to come back.

A submissive is only submissive to who she wants to submit to, or who her Master tells her to submit to. she is not a doormat, a piece of meat or a play toy for you to hound, stalk, talk rudely to or intimidate.

If you have an interest in a particular person, a good idea would be to ask around, politely and discreetly, if she is a sub (the way a person dresses does not necessarily mean anything); ask someone who knows her for an introduction to her (if she is single); and talk to her as if you were talking to your co-workers (have some respect).

If she is interested, she will say so. If she is not, she will say that, too. And you NEED to respect that, as well.

Don't ever think that you can just grab someone's breasts, ass or hair, pat or paddle someone as they walk past, make suggestive or lewd comments, or join in ANY play that you haven't been given explicit prior permission from.

Negotiations

This information is not to be considered as all encompassing, or even gospel. It is meant as a general guide to negotiating with a partner and to give you a place to start. I will use the male form for the Top and the female form for the bottom, but only for the purpose of ease in explanation. I have no prejudice either way. And I will talk mostly about this from the Dominant's point of view. But this can work for either male or female, Top or bottom. And although there may be a difference, I will use Top, Dominant and Master interchangeably, as well as submissive, bottom and slave, for purposes of this article. All of this information is my opinion and should not be mistaken for legal, religious or medical advice. And it can be used for any real life negotiating.

First Meeting
When you first walk in to a gathering or get off the Internet and go to R/T pursuits of your interest, things may seem a bit overwhelming for you, whether you're a Top or a bottom. And when you decide to "make the move" how should you begin?

Well, like in most real life situations, try honesty, sincerity and courtesy. I heard a story a while back about a guy who walked into a bar, saw a girl that he knew was a submissive. He bought her a drink and while talking to his friends, told the girl to go to his car and get him his Blackberry.

That's fine if the submissive were his submissive. Otherwise, it's rude. First rule: A submissive is only submissive to those she chooses to submit to, and a slave is only a slave to her Master and those that her Master chooses for her to submit to.

It doesn't take much to get a relationship started. Have some confidence and talk. Most times, the submissive is looking for a Dominant in the same places that the Dominant is looking for a submissive. It's just a matter of finding the right one for you.

It is my belief that in our lifestyle our cards are out on the table faster than in the vanilla world. So maybe we proceed just a little faster. But we usually find out if we are compatible long before those in the vanilla world. If you are polite, then the conversation may get started quicker. If you're nasty, there's probably someone that's right for you, too, but they are probably fewer and farther between. So, rule number two: Be polite.

Now, this page isn't about "How to Get a Date", but it all starts the same way: you talk; you get to know each other; you make plans to talk again. And since trust is our most important asset, rule number three: Be honest.

Just to get a date for the Saturday night play party is no reason to lie. If you're not into the things that she's into, then say so. If she's not interested in what you are, then it's better to find out now and move on as friends, than to try and force something and have a fight that encompasses the whole community, later. And you don't have to say that you're a fighter pilot or a heart surgeon to impress a submissive. Or vice-versa. Most times, our actions speak the loudest. Show her that you are a Dominant. Act in an honorable manner. Command respect, don't demand it. And if it looks like things are working out for you, then it's time to move on to the next step.

What Now?
Most times, some form of negotiation starts at the outset. But the true negotiating - the dos and don'ts, the hard and soft limits and the direction that you want the relationship to go, will probably not start until the participants get to know each other better.

Some people get into this lifestyle or look for partners based on their "studies" of S/M through short stories, novels, magazine articles, the Internet or some other form of fiction. If you believe everything you read in the chat rooms or the latest best-selling paperback, you're likely to be disappointed. Know what you want. Listen to what she wants. Success is more likely when the conversations and negotiations are longer and more in-depth.

When we start negotiating, we let our partner know what it is that we expect from the relationship and find out what she expects in return. Does it fit our plans? Is that what I want? Are any of these things "Deal Breakers"?

We let her know what our limits are and find out about hers. We talk about our self, but we need to listen when she's talking about herself. We state our levels of knowledge and understanding and try to find out hers. Are we compatible? Is this what we want?

OK, now we need to establish some rules. I'm all for putting things on paper. It makes it very clear what's expected and what's tolerated and what is not. How much training is needed? What kind of punishment will there be? What are the rewards? Once you start putting things on paper, everybody knows what to expect and nothing comes as a surprise.

I have a friend who went into an already formed heterosexual relationship as a beta slave. The couple already knew each other and had some set rules. Well, two days into this relationship, she was being punished for doing something that she didn't know was a "don't". Nobody told her. They expected that she knew, since, my goodness, they knew! The three of them talked a bit more, but she could never get things on paper, so she asked for her freedom and moved on.

This process gets the participants to agree to work within boundaries to see if they both accept the situation. Sometimes, a lot of discussion and changes need to take place for both parties to feel comfortable. This process may take weeks.

M/s, D/s, fetish and leather relationships can be as varied as the types of play that these people like to participate in.

Is There More?

Painfully so! Once you've gotten to this step, the relationship is not automatic. I like to recommend that the next step is to contract the slave.

My approach to contracts varies with the individual and what it is that they want and what it is that I want. What works in one situation may not necessarily work in another.

The first contract should be short - One month, tops. At the end of a month I find that it's usually necessary to make changes, where applicable. Maybe this idea didn't work. Maybe that rule wasn't stringent enough. Maybe I no longer want to decide what she should wear to work every morning.

The list can go on. So the first contract shouldn't. Then comes a second contract - maybe for another month ... maybe for three months, depending on the amount of changes needed to be made. After the three month contract, go to a six month or a year, or make it permanent if very few or no changes needed to be made the first and second times.

As I stated earlier, we put most of our cards on the table immediately and we need to live in the same incestuous community with all of the people that are potential partners. Therefore, it's extremely important to be honest, polite and sincere.

The following information was taken from the Society of Janus web page and offers some hints for both Tops and bottoms to use when negotiating.

Some General Rules for Dominants and submissives:

Ten Rules for Dominants

1 - Be patient! Until you enter into a contract with a submissive, you have no more right to order him/her around than does anyone else. Give your bottom time to get to know you and what

you are like. Finesse and subtlety are major elements of dominance. Similarly, strength and gentleness go hand in hand. The sensitivity and awareness (or lack thereof) that you show in the real world is likely to be repeated in the playroom.

2 - Be humble. You may be God's/Goddess' gift to the world, but no one needs to hear it or wants to hear it. You will have ample opportunities to show how good you are - and plenty of opportunities to make a fool of yourself. No matter what you claim, the "real you" will show through in a scene. Don't set yourself up for a failure by developing expectations that you know you can never reach.

3 - Be open. Although the top is classically considered to be the teacher in SM, you can always learn from your bottom, no matter how inexperienced. Be willing to learn from other dominants who may have a totally different perspective from yours. Try to approach by-now-familiar trips with an attitude of wonderment and discovery. Be aware that everyone has her or his own personal style.

4 - Communicate! You are responsible for finding out basic, essential information about the people you play with, such as experience, limits, likes and dislikes, and health information. Playing SM without this knowledge is like Russian roulette. Talk about your head-space and your view of SM with your bottom, so that any uncertainties can be dealt with before you start playing. Clearly spell out roles, rules, limits, and contracts. Do not take for granted that your bottom instinctively knows the ground rules.

5 - Be honest. If you lack experience in an area that your bottom would like to experiment with, be honest about it. Your partner has a right to know that. Be honest with yourself and take your submissive only to those levels at which you are completely in control of the situation. Safety should always be the first concern, taking priority over how hot a particular scene is.

6 - Be sensitive. There's a very fine line between a sensitive, caring dominant and a self-righteous, insensitive overbearing clod. Your scene should be a creative synthesis of your needs and fantasies and your bottom's needs and fantasies. Although, on the surface, your submissive is serving you, what actually is happening is that dominant and submissive are serving each other. Earn the complete trust of your submissive and never violate or even threaten to violate that trust. His or her submission is a gift to you. Use it appropriately.

7 - Be realistic. End the scene with the bottom wanting more, not wishing there had been less. Remember that power, control, and sensitivity are the keys, not just the intensity of the stimulation. Be clear about what is fantasy, and (that it) has little to do with what works in practice. Your favorite porno picture books may be stimulating in themselves, but don't try to imitate them to the last detail.

8 - Be really dominant! Submissives are looking for someone who will take over their body and mind, not just for brute strength. Real people are wanted, not just cardboard images from cigarette ads or macho stereotypes. Your dominance enhances your whole existence. It does not cover up or substitute for other areas of your life - it is you. Make your submissive fall in love with you, and expect him or her to give him/herself up to you totally. Follow up on rules, expect obedience, and punish appropriately when it is called for. Don't shirk your responsibility to your bottom or to your sister/fellow tops. Be dependable and expect dependability. You have agreed to take the dominant role - now take it!

9 - Be healthy! Like any strenuous activity, SM requires that its participants be in top physical and emotional health. Many factors, including the amount you sleep, your eating habits, and your alcohol and drug intake affect your performance and endurance during a scene. Don't attempt to do SM when your physical or emotional energy is low. As a dominant you have a

special responsibility to be in control of yourself and on top of the scene. An attitude of "drugs and alcohol don't affect me that much... I can do it anyway" violates your submissive's trust in you and can be dangerous. If you don't want to accept the responsibilities, you shouldn't be playing the game!

10 - Have fun! After all, sex is all about having a good time. You have earned, and you are entitled to the unique, intense pleasures which come from responsible, creative SM play.

Ten Rules for Submissives
1 - Be patient! A potential top will let you know if she or he is interested in you or not. Keep in mind that your purpose as a submissive is to serve and to satisfy someone who will take into consideration the realization of your fantasies. Don't expect your top to be able to turn on like a light switch. The timing must be right for both of you.

2 - Be humble. You may be God's or Goddess' gift to the world and the most sought after prize in town, but no one needs to hear it or wants to hear it. You will have ample opportunity to show how good you are. No matter what you claim, the "real you" will show through in a scene. Don't set yourself up for failure by developing expectations that you know you and your top can never reach.

3 - Be open. You can learn something about SM and about yourself from everyone into the scene, no matter how experienced or inexperienced they are, or how dominant or submissive they are. SM is a very personal art, and an "I already know it all" attitude will make you miss valuable SM lessons and experiences, and ignore potentially valuable SM friends.

4 - Communicate! Verbalization is necessary, but at the appropriate time and in the appropriate way. Your top needs to know basic information about you, such as experiences, fantasies, health concerns, and turn-offs. But - unless it's an

emergency - wait until your top asks. Don't expect your dominant to be a mind-reader who instinctively knows your needs, wants, and limits. Your cooperation will enhance the scene for both of you.

5 - Be honest. Don't be afraid to share your needs and fantasies. Your dominant expects it. Honesty about your wants, health concerns, and turn-offs is essential to a good scene. Lying or being less than candid can only lead to problems, as the top will base the scene on inaccurate information. Besides causing problems, it can be dangerous.

6 - Be vulnerable. Your scene is a two-way street. It is not just the physical realization of your prior fantasies. If you want to limit your experience to certain physical and psychological stimulation, then contract with your top ahead of time. But don't always expect your top to be a puppet in a fantasy play you've written in your head. It's far better to let your top surprise you, to extend your limits, to take you to places (you've) never been before. When you trust your top completely, let her or him know it, and let him or her guide you into new fantasies.

7 - Be realistic. Your dominant is human, and even the most experienced tops have moments of awkwardness and indecision. Don't call attention to what you perceive as a lapse. Know the difference between reality and the fantasy world you see in books and magazines. Few tops are rich enough to afford a large dungeon with a lavish layout of equipment. Your top's equipment is expensive - respect it and don't abuse it.

8 - Be really submissive! This is the whole point. Let your dominant take you over completely. Don't coach or second guess or be critical of your top. Exchange information on your special needs before the scene starts, but once it starts be quiet! If you insist on running a scene to your own specifications, then you should try being a top. You have agreed to limitations of your own power. Stay within those limitations. Respect and obey your

top and expect punishment if you don't. Accept it gracefully and cheerfully. Your top has many things to be concerned with, including your safety and what turns you on. Be loyal and dependable and enjoy your role.

9 - Be healthy! SM, like any strenuous activity, requires that its participants - both active and passive - be in top physical and emotional health. The amount that you sleep, your eating habits, your alcohol and drug intake, and everyday stress affect your response and endurance during a scene. Your dominant needs to know when your physical or emotional energy is low. No matter how tempting a scene sounds, an "I want it all now" attitude when you aren't able to give your all will leave both of you feeling let down. You serve your dominant and yourself best by staying healthy.

10 - Have fun! After all, sex is all about having a good time. You have earned, and you are entitled to, the unique, intense pleasure which comes from responsible, creative SM play.

Protocols

First let Me say that in My perception of what umbrella the BDSM community covers there are several things to include when talking about Protocol or Codes of Conduct. BDSM, to Me, represents the entire SM/leather/fetish communities. Leather protocol and codes of conduct can be very different than what you are actually looking for. Leather protocols, in My opinion, refer mostly to the way the old motorcycle club, gay leathermen, Old Guard, GLBT (Gay, Lesbian, Bisexual, Transgendered) folk and others handle protocol's. Fetish Protocol refers to a just as varied group, which includes spanko's, rubber enthusiasts, foot fetishists, etc...

SM protocol is what most people mean when they ask for BDSM or Leather protocols and codes of conduct.

That is not to say that if you are interested in one of those other things that I am against it. Rather, what I'm trying to say is that if you are interested in "Leather Protocol" or "Leather Codes of Conduct", you won't find it here. Nor will you find fetish protocols here. I live by SM protocols. So that is what I know and that is what I will try to briefly touch on.

Sometimes people get into a belief that they are learning proper SM protocols because they went to a Leather Protocol educational class. Then they come out feeling alienated or confused, because I know I have, having been to many BDSM parties over many years that were high protocol parties and yet I have never experienced a lot of the things that I heard at a Leather Protocol educational course.

Now, please try and remember that this is not to be considered as all encompassing, or even as gospel. It is meant as a general guide to making sure that when you attend a BDSM play party or interact at a BDSM munch or with others that do WIITWD (What it is that we do), you will at least have a little background and knowledge so you don't feel like a fool, out of place or that you're going to embarrass yourself.

I have always considered WIITWD as BDSM and My involvement has been in the BDSM scene, not just SM or Leather or Fetish, so that is the way I will relate this page. I will also write from the Dominant's point of view, because that's what I am. I won't try to explain every point of view from every politically correct angle, but this can work for either male or female, Top or bottom. And although there is a difference, I will use Top, Dominant and Master almost interchangeably, as well as submissive, bottom and slave, for purposes of this article. I will also use the male form for the Top and the female form for the bottom. Again, this is strictly for the sake of the article and simplicity and is not to be mistaken for anyone thinking that I do not believe in or agree with any other types of situations. And all of this information is My opinion and should not be mistaken for legal, religious or medical advice.

Part of this material comes from other articles I've written, so you know it's not just deja vu!

What's first?
When you first walk in to a BDSM gathering or get off the Internet and go to R/T pursuits of your interest, things may seem a bit overwhelming for you, whether you're a Top or a bottom. And the first question is, "How should I behave?"

Well, like in most real life situations, try honesty, sincerity and courtesy as a good place to start. And be polite.

Is there more?
BDSM is, by definition, about procedures and protocol. Although there are no written "SOP's" (because as varied as the population is, is as varied as the protocols may be), there are several behaviors that are standards for the community.

Read and be familiar with the rules of the party You attend.

All play should be consensual.

Normal scene etiquette is a must (i.e., Do not interfere with a scene, do not invade scene space, etc).

Do not touch another individual without first getting permission.

Do not touch another's toys or toy bags without first getting permission.

Even if you have permission to touch it, ask again before swinging, cracking or popping it.

NEVER touch a collared person's collar!

Before talking to anyone wearing a collar, try to find their Dominant first, and ask His permission.

Keep conversation, laughter and comments to a minimum in the play areas.

Do not monopolize the equipment.

Do NOT join a scene unless specifically asked to do so!

Clean up after your scene.

Honest, open and respectful negotiation is acceptable.

You are expected to know that other people might ask you to play. There is a wide variety of play that is possible.

The person who asks is expected to be polite, and to respect the collar of anyone who is collared, or to respect the relationships of other couples or leather families.

If you want to play with the person who asks, you are welcome to say, "Yes."

If you do not want to play with the other person, you are expected to say, "No."

If you do not want to play with the other person, but say, "Yes," or do not "safeword" (if that is what is necessary to prevent unwanted play), then you have violated their trust. If you ask someone to play, and they say, "No," you are expected to respect their wishes.

Safewords are considered part of normal scene etiquette.

Not all participants are open with their families and employers about their BDSM involvement, sexual orientation or personal fetishes, so information about other participants is not to be shared without the direct consent of the person in question.

Never take pictures without the consent of all parties involved. Do not mention proper names or describe a person in such a way that their identity may be determined, without consent of that person.

Never give out addresses of play parties except to your sponsored guests (with the permission of the host)..

Never give out e-mail addresses without consent of that person.

Do not discuss ("out") the alternative activities or preferences of participants to any person, organization or business not directly involved with the participant.

Is that all?

Who are you kidding! Besides for the above, there are many other rules of conduct or normal scene etiquette and behavior that will enhance your chances of being accepted. People that are usually held in the highest regard are not self-seeking. They are very approachable and will usually welcome questions, so long as they are not in "High Protocol" (specific rules used between consenting couples that tend to exclude them from the crowd for a variety of reasons). Do not be embarrassed to ask questions, but avoid asking them immediately preceding or following a scene or when they are engaged in other conversation.

Consider that any BDSM gathering may be a chance for people who may or may not practice protocols during "business hours" as a place where they can, so always be on your best behavior, regardless of your perception of the mood and atmosphere.

Can I go now?

Almost. Sometimes you might find that there are quirks or intricacies that you don't understand. Sometimes, people use varied protocols in dealing with their significant other. Best friends might use different protocols with their respective submissive's and still go out together.

Some of these variables include:

Being the driver verses having a chauffeur.

Chivalry verses chauvinism.

Polite verses demanding.

Micromanaging verses allowing plenty of leeway.

Controlling her diet verses putting her in charge of Yours.

Hand signals verses verbal commands.

Walking with her to your right and slightly behind you verses making her clear the path by walking out in front.

Honorifics - The choice of what You want her to call You and other Dominants. From the online "Master" and those that have no business using the term to the person who has earned the title, "Master" for a skill or ability they have proved through the years, to "Sir" or whatever else You want to be called.

As many people as there are is as many different protocols that you may find. What's good for you and what you want to incorporate into your relationship is how You decide Your personal protocols.

No one has ever gotten mad at another person for being polite. If you say, "Sir" or "Ma'am" when you talk to others, you're heading in the right direction. If you follow normal scene etiquette for SM when in an SM atmosphere, you will do just fine. If you are in a Leather atmosphere, find out what leather protocols are. If you are in a special interest or fetish environment, use their protocols. If it is inappropriate, someone will certainly tell you what protocol is being practiced. But if you stick to SM events and use SM protocols, codes of conduct, rules of behavior or normal scene etiquette, you will do just fine.

And don't mistake "Leather Protocol" with "SM Protocol". It can be confusing!

Safecall Guide and Outline

What you should know about Safecalls

Safecalls is another subject that gets mentioned, but doesn't get discussed in detail. I've received such good input that it became necessary to give this subject its own chapter. In this day and age of internet anonymity and kidnappings shielded by claims of consensual S/m play, a safecall is an important tool. A tool to be used when meeting someone new, someone for the first time, or someone met through an internet encounter.

What Is a Safecall?

A Safecall is a person who you trust, who you can give information to about the who, what and where's of your meeting, who will keep up with you in case of an emergency.

Who Needs a Safecall?

Anyone who is meeting someone for the first time or anyone getting together with someone they met at a munch, party or meeting that they are going to have their first private encounter with.

But I'm a Big, Bad Dom Type

How do you know that the 5'2", 110 lb. blonde you got a picture of on the internet is not really four drunken hillbilly rednecks that enjoy beating the shit out of "perverts and queers"?
There's no way that I believe that everyone I spoke with on the internet is exactly who they claim to be. Do you?

Who Should You Pick to be Your Safecall?

Anyone that you trust. Someone that will be there for you and is not afraid to call 911. Someone who is smart enough to realize that all encounters don't end up good.

What information should You give Your Safecall person?

When meeting someone over the internet, you already have their screen name.

Get the full name of the person you are going to meet.
Get their phone number
Their driver's license number
Their address
Place of employment
References

Some people may or may not want to give out all of this information. Remember: If something goes really wrong, someone needs to know how to find you. People who are not willing to give most of this information, probably have something to hide.

Once I Have This Information, What Do I Do?
Before meeting with the new person, set up your Safecall. Give the Safecall person all the information you have gathered. Also, set up a code phrase, in case things get out of hand and there's no way for you to tell that to your Safecall person without giving it away. Something simple, like "Yes, my mother knows." It's obscure and doesn't sound to the abuser like a negative statement.

As soon as you meet with the person, call your Safecall. Tell them you've arrived, and make sure they have the information. Call again two hours later to let them know you are still safe. (Meals and idle chit chat don't usually last more than two hours). If you met at a restaurant and leave to go to their house, or somewhere else, call again with the new location. It also provides a time line. Again make sure your Safecall has the information. Call again in two hours. Either you are about to play or have finished a two hour session. Either way, two hours is a good limit for a first encounter. Any worthwhile Dom or sub should respect that.

If you are staying, call again in two hours. If you plan on sleeping there, let your Safecall know and be sure to call before going to bed and upon waking up. If you're going to a motel, call once you get there.

If you give the new person the name and room number of the hotel, be sure to call your Safecall every 2 hours until you go to bed and again when you wake up. Just because a person is sweet and polite at the restaurant or their house, doesn't mean they're not opportunists. Bundy and Dahmer were charming!

Most first time encounters end up fine. Maybe the people don't get along, but it is not dangerous for either participant. However, the ones that do end up bad, end up very bad. As we always say in the SSC lifestyle, "Err on the side of caution". It's always better to be safe than sorry...or dead. BDSM is NOT abuse.

I'm not making judgment calls on sleeping with people you've just met, only to say to remember to practice safer sex if you choose to engage in that behavior with a brand new partner that you just met.

What should the Safecall Person Know or Do?
There are any number of different items that could be useful in helping someone to meet with a new partner. When a person writes to you to ask you to be their Safecall, if you are not sure you can do it, point them towards someone who can.

I used to think that if they would not follow these guidelines to the letter, than I would not be there Safecall. However, when a person most needs Me is not the time to stand on ceremony or pride. Whatever you can get is better than not getting anything if, god forbid, something should go awry.

Have the person writing to you give you their phone number, and give them a call. You need to protect yourself, as well.

Tell them that they should get certain information from the person they are going to meet. These things are listed above and outlined in the template below. Tell them to give this information to you, too.

Once you have this information, try to get an idea of what they are planning on doing, where they are planning on going and how long it is supposed to last. Have a notebook available to write this information down next to their other information. If they are willing, help them set up a plan if they don't already have one. Once you have done this, get their name and address. Ask for pictures of one or both people, if possible, should the need to give this information to the authorities arise.

Come up with a code phrase, such as, "Yes, my mother knows". It's obscure enough not to raise suspicion and doesn't sound to the abuser like a negative comment or statement. If you hear the code phrase, call 911.

Do not attempt to go and save the person yourself. If your caller fails to make contact at a specified time, assume the worst and notify police. Most meetings go off without a hitch. Most times you will feel almost bored by the monotony of the calls. Usually, if nothing else, you will gain another friendship through the conversations.

A template for you to use is below. Leave room for other information you may be able to gather and feel free to copy and paste the template for you to use in your notebook.

Safecall Work Sheet

Caller's Name:
Caller's Address:
Caller's Phone number:
Caller's Driver's License number:
Other Person's Name:
Other Person's Address:
Other Person's Phone number:
Other Person's Driver's License number:
Other Person's References:
Other Person's Place of employment:
Code Phrase:
Time of meeting:
Place of meeting:
Date of meeting:
2nd Time of meeting:
2nd Place of meeting:
3rd Time of meeting:
3rd Place of meeting:
Time of 1st Check in:
Time of Next Check in:
Time of Next Check in:
Time of Next Check in:
Time of Next Check in:
Time date completed:
Notes:

Thank you for being a part of this important endeavor.

Whip Presentation and Demonstration
© 2013 Sir Bamm!

I am a certified Master with signal whips. I can use two whips, either two three-footers or a three-footer and a four-footer, simultaneously, and can do so on multiple "victims". I have been into What It Is That We Do, in one form or another, since the late '70s, although in public settings, since only around 1990. I have given this presentation to SAADE, at NLA's TLP, at Kinky Aggies, and portions of it I've given as part of My class for the SAADE Mentors Program. I've done numerous private teaching sessions; I've given it for TOL; and most recently for Central Texas Boys of Leather (CTBOL).

Part one is the presentation. Part two is a demonstration in which I use three submissives of different heights. I show the different markings that the signal whips can make on the different submissives. I then do a short scene using a single tail in each hand, and all three submissives, at the same time.

Definition:
Whip n.
1. A pliable lash used in whipping. (Riverside/Webster's II Dictionary)
2. A flexible thong or lash used for driving animals. (Dictionary.com)
3. A BDSM play toy. (Sir Bamm!)

Note: Even though floggers and "cats" are often called whips, for purposes of this presentation, "whip" will be used to describe single tails, only.

A brief history of whips:
Whips have been used for centuries. Written records show that Ancient Egyptians used whips to drive slaves, and as a sign of authority. Here, in Texas, in the Old West, whips were used to drive cattle and often times used in fights. Whips have even been

used in Hollywood movies, such as Batman Returns, Raiders of The Lost Ark, and Mask of Zorro. But that's not all. In Australia, Mexico, during the Roman Empire, and in many other places and times, whips have been used as symbols of authority, strength, courage, and to drive animals and men. And famous whip cracker's, such as Snowy Baker and Douglas Fairbanks, have used whips for show, and for showing off.

Different types of whips:
Stock whip -- long rigid handle, attached thong, fall, cracker.
Bull whip -- short rigid handle, attached thong, fall, and cracker.
Pocket snake -- thong (filled with shot inside a sack, instead of having a handle), fall, and cracker.
Signal whip -- thong (filled with shot), cracker.

Reasons for using a whip in BDSM play:
Power -- (For Top) shows skill (For bottom) shows conviction.
Uniqueness -- Nothing else feels or sounds like a whip.
Sensation -- Breeze, slight sting, burning heat, and everything in between.
Smaller toy bag.

How I got into whips:
I first started with a whip around 1993 with My first slave. she was totally into pain and I couldn't find anything to hurt her enough until I hit her with a single tail. Back then there weren't a whole lot of places to learn about whips, and information wasn't readily available or easy to come by. I learned on My own, making plenty of mistakes along the way. And I started with 4 plait whips.
Since most of our play in those days was limited to private play, or in people's homes, the longer whips weren't practical.
At first, I would hold the whip further down the thong. Then I started cutting the handles off. I moved in and out of the lifestyle for a few years and when I came back, I learned about signal whips.

I practiced on light switches (the electrical kind) and items hanging off the edge of furniture, and finally started on people again. Sometimes, just for practice, I will still take a bulletin board, put nine business cards on it in a tic-tac-toe pattern and practice making light marks on the cards rather than striking to knock them off the board. This helps Me with pinpoint accuracy. Also, I do not recommend practicing on light switches (the electrical kind) for long periods of time or You will be replacing crackers regularly.

My preference is the 8 plait, 3 or 4 foot, signal whip. And My specialty is using two different length whips, one in each hand, and making them strike the exact location I am aiming at. Besides for My! t, whips are My favorite toy.

How I got into using two whips at once:
This was more by accident than anything else. In 1998, during a softball coach's clinic that I attended, the instructors were showing us how to teach girls the way to throw the ball with speed and accuracy. The biggest deal they made was that if we tried using our weak hand to throw we would know what it was like to "throw like a girl". I learned to use My weak hand as good as My strong hand.

Soon after, while working with My whips at home, My strong arm was getting tired so I took the signal whip in My other hand and started cracking it that way. It wasn't quite as easy as learning to throw a softball, but it opened up possibilities that I never imagined.

Different plaits:
The plaiting is the number of pieces of leather braided into the whip. One way to tell how many plaits a whip has is to look at the knot on the whip and count all the tiny triangles in the first row down the thong. 4 plait (IMO) is junk. Those are the ones commonly found in tack stores or novelty shops. 8 plait is harder to treat than higher plaited whips, and the leather stays harder, longer. 12 plait is softer,

and handles much easier, is easier to control, and breaks in, and stays broken in longer with less treatment. The higher the plait, the more expensive the whip.

For example:
An 8 plait, 3-foot signal whip, in black, runs around $180.00.
An 8 plait, 4-foot, signal whip in black, runs around $195.00.
A 12 plait, 6 foot, pocket snake runs around $525.00.
12 plait, 8 foot, stock and bull whips run around $735.00.

Most of the better quality signal whips will not have more than 8 plaits. The reason for this is that a signal whip differs from a bull, stock or snake whip since it does not have a fall between the thong and the cracker. It must therefore end in 4 strands in order to attach the cracker. Anything above 8 strands would demand too many drop points (16 to 8 to 4, etc.) and would end up being inferior in quality and durability and the taper would not be as clean.

What to look for when buying a whip:
Quality of workmanship -- see that the "v" in the plaiting is in a straight line down the whip. Look to see that the cracker is braided into the fall without too much of an awkward looking connection. Using both hands in opposing directions, lightly twist the fall to make sure the leather is braided tightly. Go with the better-known companies if you're unsure. (Wheeler, David Morgan, etc.)

Sometimes the ends of the plaited leather, which are buried under the thread of the cracker, will poke out after the whip is cracked. This is not a cause for concern. The nylon used for the cracker is much more elastic than the leather used in the thong, so when the whip is cracked the threads from the nylon tend to creep out over the leather ends and allow the leather ends to poke out. A good signal whip will have three knots holding the ends to ensure that the whip does not unravel.

David Morgan recommends that You leave the ends poking out, and not trim them off.

Size -- Size does matter. But bigger isn't always better. What works best for You and Your play area is the best size.

Caring for your whips:
Never use light liquid treatments. And never use neatsfoot oil. Neatsfoot and other largely popular leather dressings contain animal fats which provide an atmosphere conducive to the growth of fungus and bacteria, which is very bad when being used in blood related games, and can weaken the leather over time. The lightest thing you should ever use is baseball glove leather treatment. I recommend Pecard Leather Dressing.
Note: When the signal whip or pocket snake is brand new, do not excessively bend the thong. You could break the sack that holds the shot. Once the whip is broken in well and the dressing has been applied numerous times, the thong will bend easier and there is less chance of breaking the sack.
When the fluff on the end of the cracker wears down to the first knot, you can either undo the knot or cut it off, to form a new, second fluff. Since most of the better quality signal whips have three knots, using Your whip until this happens is perfectly fine. However, when it wears down to the second knot, that's the time that the cracker should be replaced.

The physics of whips:
The speed of the cracker can reach supersonic velocity (approx.1400 feet per second). Since the cracker reaches supersonic velocity, it creates a minor sonic boom.
F=MA (force equals mass times acceleration). (I have no idea what this has to do with this presentation, but an engineer told Me that, so I put it in).

Creating the single tail scene:
Whips are made out of leather. Use the entire whip. Around the neck, rub down the back, press against the bottom's lips,

etc...Warm up Your bottom (and Your play partner, too). Do not just go straight to drawing blood.

Single tail scene's can be as varied as the effect they have on the bottom. They can be erotic without ever touching the bottom. They can mark, scratch or be welt producing. Or they can turn Your masochist into a hunk of chopped meat. Remember, too, that some masochists and bottoms are not submissives, and some submissives are not masochists. Adjust your play accordingly.

The rhythm of the strokes can be used to warm up Your play partner by building a layer of sensation. Allow the bottom to react to the impact, absorb it, and then recover from it. Sometimes, the reaction is slower than that of a flogger or crop, since the crack and the movement are so quick, it takes a little time to react. The whip does not have to crack to be effective.

Safety:
Whips are extremely dangerous. They can be as dangerous to You as they are to Your bottom. Remember when swinging a whip, the whip will follow its own path. It is extremely easy to break skin with a whip. Whips were made to make noise. They travel at the speed of sound. They do not like being stopped short by people's bodies getting in their way. When first learning how to use a whip wear eye protection, thick clothing and if necessary, a helmet.

NEVER use a whip on another living being until you have mastered it.

If blood is drawn, dress the wound and clean the whip. If the cracker is made of leather it is almost impossible to fully sterilize it. Therefore, be sure to use, at the very minimum, hydrogen peroxide, alcohol or an antibacterial soap. Nylon crackers are the easiest to clean and a simple hydrogen peroxide and water solution, an alcohol and water solution, or an antibacterial soap will not damage the nylon, and is very effective in cleaning.

The aerosolizing of blood can contact others in the area of the scene. I have never heard of anyone getting a blood related disease from the aerosolized blood droplets, but I don't know if any studies were done on the subject, nor do I know a whole lot of people who want to get hit with blood droplets anyway. Insure there is enough space to swing Your whip (twice the length of the whip). Pick the right whip for You. Longer whips are not always better whips, or better whips for You.

Clean and disinfect the whip between uses, and most importantly between bottoms. Clean and dress any wounds to the bottom.

Basic Strokes:
Posture is relatively important when first learning how to crack a single tail. Start by balancing yourself on both feet, legs spread about shoulder distance apart, knees slightly bent, with your striking arm shoulder facing your target, and your face and extremities well out of the way. Hold the whip with the knot in the palm of Your hand allowing the whip to swivel in your hand as you move it to reduce the stress and bending near the knob, where the shot sack is. And remember that the whip will follow it's own path. After You have mastered the whip You can move around, dance or stand on one leg.

Archer -- simple two-handed stroke that is easy to learn.
Over hand -- controlled stroke.
Backhand -- Basically, an easy stroke. Covers a lot of area. Also used to set distance and accuracy, and to set up combinations.
Forehand -- Very showy.
Back Crack or Circus Crack-- Mostly used with longer whips. If using only 3 or 4 foot signal whips, there is no reason to use this stroke unless You are taming lions.
Circle crack -- over head back crack. Very showy, very loud and extremely painful if contact is made.

Whipiquette:
Be aware that cracking your whip at a public play space can distract others and may also draw a crowd.
Ask before handling someone else's whip (or other play items).
Ask before cracking someone else's whip (or other play items).
Be aware that a whip can leave marks that can last a very long time.

References:
www.davidmorgan.com
Singletails for Sensualists and Sadists by Marc B.
Singletail by Master Al
Riverside/Webster's II Dictionary
Dictionary.com

9 Levels of submission

Within S/M, different people use the words "submissive", "bottom" and "slave" to mean different things. When a person says, "I want to be your slave," sometimes they only mean that they want to be tied up and spanked. Many ProDom(me)s routinely refer to their (usually not genuinely submissive) clients as "slaves". At the other extreme, there are people who want to be full-time personal servants, and who truly want to exist solely for their Dom(me)'s use, pleasure and convenience. And as many definitions as there are, there are just as many shades in between these two extremes.

For an alpha slave, the definition of "number 8" is what I look for.

The following is intended as a loose classification. It was written by Diane Vera and published in *Lesbian S/M Safety Manual*, from Alyson Press, Copyright 1984 and 1988. Numerous attempts were made to contact the author.

1. THE OUTRIGHT NON-SUBMISSIVE MASOCHIST or KINKY SENSUALIST.
Not into servitude, humiliation or giving up control; just pain and/or spiced-up sensuality, on the masochist's own terms and for the masochist's own direct pleasure (i.e. turned on solely/mainly by one's own bodily sensations rather than by being "used" to gratify one's partner's sadism).

2. PSEUDO-SUBMISSIVE NON-SLAVE.
Not into even playing "slave," but into other "submissive" role-playing, e.g. schoolteacher scenes, infantilism, "forced" transvestitism. Usually into humiliation, but NOT into servitude, even in play. Dictates the scene to a large degree.

3. PSEUDO-SUBMISSIVE PLAY SLAVE.
Likes to play at being a slave; likes to feel subservient; may in some cases like to feel one is being "used" to gratify partner's

sadism; may even really serve the dominant in some ways, but only on the "slave's" own terms. Dictates the scene to a large degree; often fetishistic (e.g. foot worshippers).

4. TRUE SUBMISSIVE NON-SLAVE.

Really gives up control (only temporarily and within agreed-upon limits), but gets her/his main satisfaction from aspects of submission other than serving or being used by the dominant. Usually turned on by suspense, vulnerability, and/or giving up reasonability. Doesn't dictate the scene except in very general terms, but still seek mainly her/his own direct/pleasure (rather than getting one's pleasure mainly from pleasing the dominant).

5. TRUE SUBMISSIVE PLAY SLAVE.

Really gives up control (though only temporarily; only during brief "scenes" and within limits) and gets main satisfaction from serving/being used by dominant-but only for FUN purposes, usually erotic. May/may not be into pain. If so, is turned on by pain indirectly, i.e. enjoys being the object of one's partner's sadism, on which the submissive places very few requirements or restrictions.

6. UNCOMMITTED SHORT-TERM BUT MORE THAN PLAY SEMI-SLAVE.

Really gives up control (usually within limits); wants to serve and be used by the dominant; wants to provide practical/non erotic as well as fun/erotic services; but only when the "slave" is in the mood. May even act as a full-time slave for, say, several days at a time, but is free to quit at any time (or at the end of the agreed upon several days). May or may not have long-term relationship with one's Mistress, but, either way, the "slave" has the final say over when she will serve.

7. PART-TIME CONSENSUAL-BUT REAL SLAVE.

Has an ongoing commitment to an owner/slave relationship and regards oneself as the dominant's property at all times. Wants to obey and please Dom(me) in all aspects of life-practical/non erotic and fun/erotic. Devotes most of time to other commitments (e.g. job) but Dom(me) has first pick of the slave's free time.

8. FULL-TIME LIVE IN CONSENSUAL SLAVE.
Within no more than a few broad limits/requirements, the slave regards herself/himself as existing solely for the Dom(me)'s pleasure/well being. Slave in turn expects to be regarded as a prized possession. Not much different from the situation of the traditional housewife, except that within the S/M world the slave's position is more likely to be fully consensual, especially if the slave is male. Within the S/M world, a full time "slave" arrangement is entered into with an explicit awareness of the magnitude carefully, with more awareness of the magnitude of power that is being given up, and hence is usually entered into much more carefully, with more awareness of the possible dangers, and with much clearer and more specific agreements than usually precede the traditional marriage.

9. CONSENSUAL TOTAL SLAVE WITH NO LIMITS.
A common fantasy ideal which probably doesn't exist in real life (except in authoritarian religious cults and other situations where the "consent" is induced by brainwashing and/or social or economic pressures, and hence isn't fully consensual). A few S/M purists will insist that you aren't really a slave unless you're willing to do absolutely anything for your Dom(me), with no limits at all. I've met a few people who claimed to be no-limit slaves, but in all cases I have reason to doubt the claim.

BDSM vs. Abuse

Safe, sane and consensual play is the standard of the organized SM community; it relies on the use of a "safeword" that allows the bottom to stop the action at any time. Without informed consent, it is not SM, it is abuse.

SM always requires free, informed consent of all parties involved. A propensity to violence is therefore a fallacy, since the only time we engage in SM behavior is with our partners.

SM partners take great care to make sure that their activities are as safe as possible. SM does not feel like it looks.

SM partners do not have to apologize to each other. Instead, they are happy and satisfied. Unlike abuse or violence, where one party has not given informed consent to the activity. Children cannot give informed consent, therefore are never a part of SM activity.

SM happens in the context of an erotic relationship. Just as context helps differentiate between an organized boxing match and a street brawl.

Technical reference material and participation in organized groups provide the tell-tale signs for differences between SM and violence or abuse.

Tell-tale signs of the differences between Probable Cause and Consensual BDSM:

a) Signs of significant preparation. e.g. Adult toys, music, bondage furniture, lubricants and safety supplies.
b) Restraints. Abusers tend to restrain their victims with fear and intimidation, not safety clips and quick releases.
c) We call 911 in a medical emergency, not when there are loud noises.

d) The availability of mentors, reference materials and technical guides.

NOTE: The above information was gathered from the *NCSF Law Enforcement Information Project of Consensual SM Activities*. The purpose of which is to provide law enforcement with a basic understanding about adults whose sexuality and lovemaking includes SM activities and to provide them with information to assist when they encounter an SM event.

To further the idea of the differences between SM and abuse, I found other information that may also be useful when dealing with LE.

1. SM rarely results in facial marks or marks that are received on the forearms (defensive marks).
2. There is usually an even pattern of marks if it is SM, indicating the bottom held quite still during the stimulation.
3. The marks are often quite well-defined when inflicted by a toy like cane or whip, whereas in abuse there are blotches of soft-tissue bruising, randomly distributed.
4. The common areas for SM stimulation is on the buttocks, thighs, back, breasts, or the genitals. The fleshy parts of the body can be stimulated intensely and pleasurably.

Two Definitions of Abuse

"An abusive relationship is one in which substantial physical, mental, or emotional harm is inflicted, that is not temporary in nature, and is not clearly compensated for by positive and loving experiences over a long period of time." -- louise, 1997

"Acts inflicted on a person without their freely given consent." -- Leather Leadership Conference III, Statement on Abuse, San Francisco, April 16-18, 1999

D/s or Abuse?

D/s is about the building of a trusting relationship between two consenting adult partners.

D/s is about the mutual respect demonstrated between two enlightened people.

D/s is about a shared enjoyment of controlled erotic pain and/or humiliation for mutual pleasure.

D/s is about loving each other completely and without reservation in an alternate way.

D/s frees a submissive from the restraints of years of vanilla conditioning to explore a buried part of herself.

D/s builds self-esteem as a person discovers and embraces their long hidden sexuality.

Abuse is about the breach of trust between an authority figure and the person in their care.

Abuse is about the lack of respect that one person demonstrates to another person.

Abuse is about a form of out-of-control physical violence and/or personal or emotional degradation of the submissive.

Abuse is hurtful. It is also very damaging emotionally and spiritually to the submissive.

Abuse binds a submissive to a lonely and solitary life of shame, fear and secrecy... imprisoning her very soul.

Abuse shatters and destroys a person's self-esteem and leaves self-hatred in its place.

One Possible slave Contract

There are as many different possible "contracts" as there are Ds relationships. This is but one that you can use as a guide.

NOTE: *It is illegal to actually suggest ownership of another person. The contract below is for entertainment purposes only. No such contract actually ever existed.*

i, (name of slave), with a free mind and an open heart; do request of Sir that He accept the enslavement of my will unto His and to take me into His care and guidance, that Wwe may grow together in love, trust and mutual respect. The satisfaction of His wants, desires, and whims are consistent with my desire as a slave to be found pleasing to Him.

To that end, i offer Him use of my time, talents, and abilities.

Further, i ask, in sincere humility, that, as my Master, He accept the keeping of my body for the fulfillment and enhancement of my sexual, spiritual, emotional, and intellectual needs. To achieve this, He may have unfettered use of my body any time, any place, in front of anyone; to keep or to give away, with or without His presence, as He will determine; with respect to my stated limits.

i ask that He guide me in any sexual, sensual, or scene-related behavior, both with, and separate, from Him, in such a way as to further my growth as an individual and a slave.

It is agreed that grievances may be aired in a respectful manner, and that there are to be no secrets from one another.

It is accepted and agreed that i will be the sole property of Sir. That all contact with other Dominants in a public or private environment shall adhere strongly to the protocol of respect for that Dominant and of Sir's property, and that any desire to be "played" by another be first brought by the slave to Sir for consideration. The permission, or denial of such permission, shall lie solely with Sir, and His decision is non-negotiable.

In this vein, i hereby agree:

To obey His commands to the best of my ability.
To strive to overcome feelings of guilt or shame, jealousy, and all inhibitions that interfere with my capability to serve Him and limit my growth as His slave.
To maintain honest and open communication.
To reveal thoughts, feelings, and desires with a minimum of hesitation or embarrassment.
To inform Him of wants and perceived needs, recognizing that He is the sole judge of whether or how these shall be satisfied.
To strive toward maintenance of a positive self-image and development of realistic expectations and goals.
To strive toward attaining and maintaining the health and physical attributes that would be appealing to Him.
To work with Him to become a happy and self-fulfilled M/s family.
To work against negative aspects of ego and insecurities that would interfere with advancement of these aims.
That whether or not a collar is worn, it will be inferred and implied by the signing of this contract when in scene-friendly environments, and at all other times.
my surrender as a slave is done with the knowledge that nothing asked of me will demean me as an individual, and will in no way diminish my own responsibilities toward making utmost use of my potential. In recognition of my other obligations, nothing will be required of me that will in any way damage or harm my children, nor interfere with the performance of my duties as a mother.
This, i, (slave's name), do entreat, with lucidity and the realization of what this means, both stated and implied, in the conviction that this offer will be understood in the spirit of faith, caring, esteem and devotion in which it is given.

Should either of Uus find that Oour aspirations are not being well served by this agreement, find this commitment too burdensome, or for any other reason wish to cancel, Eeither may do so by written notification to the Oother, in keeping with the consensual nature of this agreement. Wwe understand that cancellation means a cessation of the control stated and implied within this agreement.

Upon cancellation, each of Uus agrees to offer to the other His! or her reasons and to assess our new needs and situation openly and lovingly.

This agreement shall serve as the basis for an extension of Oour relationship, committed to in the spirit of loving and consensual Dominance and submission with the intention of furthering self-awareness and exploration, promoting health and happiness, and improving Bboth of our lives.

It is also agreed that this shall be the permanent Master/slave document by which Wwe both agree to adhere to and will begin on (date), and will be open ended with no expiration date.

i, (slave), offer my consent into slavery to Sir under the terms stated above, on this, the ___ day of ____, in the year ____.

(Signature of slave)

I offer My acceptance of slavery by (slave) under the terms stated above on this the ___ day of ___ in the year ____.

(Signature of Sir)

Safer Sex

Preface:
This subject does not belong here exclusively. Nor does this article need to remain secret. If you would like to share it, feel free to do so, but please give credit to the authors.

NOTE: *The author is not engaged in rendering medical, legal or other professional service. This chapter should not be considered a substitute for formal medical advice.*

Introduction:
After numerous conversations with my good friend Alpha, I decided that Safer Sex was worth a chapter of its own. The information in this chapter is taken from web sources, conversations with Alpha and from The Society for Human Sexuality.

This chapter focuses on the basics of the safer sex premise, and on how to take precautions and yet feel as much pleasure as possible. We say, "Safer Sex" rather than "Safe Sex" because no precaution is absolute or one-hundred percent effective.

Precautions may not be necessary when neither you nor your partner has anything you could transmit to each other, or you are "fluid-bonded" and are completely safe in your interactions with others. It may also not be an issue if pregnancy is not a factor. But when health and peace of mind can be enhanced by playing safely, these precautions should be considered.

Condoms:
The single most effective thing you can do to remain healthy while being sexually active is to use a latex condom. The use of condoms is for vaginal or anal intercourse. One size does not fit all and all condoms are not alike. You should experiment with different brands until you find one that you like. When putting a

condom on, pinch the tip as you unroll it to prevent air from gathering there. Roll the condom all the way down. For tight, dry or anal intercourse you should use a water-based lubricant on the outside of the condom to help keep the condom from tearing during sex and to aid in the ease, comfort and mutual pleasure from the sexual encounter. A friend of mine has also told me that he puts a small amount of lubricant inside the tip of the condom before putting it on and it helps him feel sensations better. You also need to hold onto the base of the condom as you remove yourself from your partner so it doesn't slip off, leak or remain inside your partner. The condom is much tighter on a blood-filled penis then on a flaccid one. When you use a condom it is recommended that you choose a product that contains Nonoxynol-9 to protect against the transmission of HIV and AIDS and help prevent pregnancy.

Anal and Vaginal Intercourse:
If a condom tears or falls off during intercourse, the person being penetrated should not douche. If contraceptive foam is handy it might help for him or her to use the contraceptive foam and leave it in for at least 15 minutes. It is also important to immediately remove the torn or fallen-off condom from inside the person who was penetrated. If you fear pregnancy because of a condom failure or a human error, there is a 24 hour number you can call to find out about emergency contraception. That number is 888-NOT-2-LATE.

The penetrator can give himself a little extra protection after sex by immediately urinating and then washing his penis with an anti-bacterial soap starting at the base of the penis and working his way to the tip.

From the "If I don't mention it, someone might try it" category:
A new condom needs to be used for each new encounter, with each new partner and condoms should never be used more than once. And if you're going to go from anal intercourse to vaginal intercourse, put on a new condom, as well.

Regarding Oral Sex:

Opinions differ among the experts on the use of oral barriers or condoms during penis in mouth sex. Doctors have warned that herpes can be transmitted from the genitals to the mouth and from the mouth to the genitals. But some doctors and many oral sex practitioners feel that the risk is acceptable outside of the most infectious period of herpes, which starts with the tingling sensations that precede an outbreak and continue until about two weeks after the sores go away. You can also contract bacterial infections during oral sex from someone who has Gonorrhea or other bacterial infections. Gonorrhea, however, is usually treatable with antibiotics. It is generally believed that it is not possible to transmit Syphilis from the genitals to the mouth or from the mouth to the genitals.

Some doctors go so far as to say that flossing and brushing your teeth is not recommended for an hour before you perform oral sex on someone, if your partner plans not to wear a condom or oral barrier. Their recommendations, if you're concerned about your breath, are to use a mouthwash or take breath mints.

Another good idea would be to tactfully scrutinize a new partner's genitalia before you actually engage in the oral copulation. You cannot see HIV or AIDS, but you can see genital warts, scabs and sores. This can be done by looking and feeling while all in the name of giving your partner a pleasurable feeling before you actually go down on him or her.

It is a good idea not to let new partners or one time partners ejaculate in your mouth. If you let your partner ejaculate in your mouth or you tell him not to and he does anyway, it is better to spit immediately than to swallow. And in the case he has a bacterial infection it helps to use an anti-bacterial mouthwash afterward. Your partner may also not mind kissing you as much if you rinse your mouth with mouthwash immediately after performing oral sex.

If you decide to use a condom or oral barrier for oral sex, then Nonoxynol-9 is not recommended (It just plain tastes disgusting). Saran Wrap works well for both male and female oral to genital contact or you can get oral dams from the Planned Parenthood Center at no cost. A friend of mine told me that female dams work well for analingus (or "rimming") as well; and another friend says that if he lubricates the female's side of the oral dam before oral sex, she feels the sensations much better when he performs oral sex on her.

When Using Your Hands:

Latex gloves can be worn anytime you may encounter any bodily fluid. You can also wear latex gloves just to be "safer" than "sorry". Removing latex gloves after a scene and discarding them in a conveniently placed bio-hazard container (which is also called a zip lock bag) or a "sharps container" (which is designed for "sharps" - needles, scalpels and bloody disposable toys and gloves) and allows you to not have to leave the scene when you are done playing. If you have cuts or wounds on your hands you should wear latex gloves. Latex gloves should also be worn if you are planning on putting your fingers, hand or fist into your partner's anus.

The proper way to remove a latex glove is to start at the top, by your wrist, and pull the first glove inside out from wrist to fingers. While still in contact with the glove's fingers, use your exposed-hand/still-gloved-fingers to remove the other glove in the same fashion, pulling the second glove off inside out and then wrapping the second over the first as you completely remove the first from your hand, so that whatever is on the outside of the glove becomes caught on the inside of the removed gloves.

If you've had your ungloved fingers in someone's vagina or anus, or had someone ejaculate on your bare hands, you should wash your hands thoroughly with hot water and anti-bacterial soap before bringing your hands near your eyes or mouth and before touching someone else's genitalia.

Latex Alternatives:
If you or your partner is allergic to latex, there are non-latex alternatives. A non-latex glove is available at most pharmacies, although not quite as "safer". If you cannot use latex oral barriers, then Saran Wrap does a good job as an alternative. There are also non-latex condoms available at most drug stores.

Risks:
Preseminal fluid, or pre-cum, may contain the HIV virus if your partner is infected. If you are concerned about becoming infected from pre-cum while performing oral sex you can either use a condom or other oral barrier or you can perform oral sex without putting the head of your partner's penis in your mouth.

Hepatitis A can also be transmitted from the mouth to the anus during analingus.

The risk of transmitting HIV is lower for unprotected oral sex than for unprotected anal or vaginal sex. The risk is much lower for the person having oral sex performed on them than for the person doing the performing. The risk is reduced even more if you do not swallow the ejaculate. And it is reduced even more than that if your partner does not ejaculate in your mouth.

For the person giving the oral sex, the risk of contracting HIV is also lowered if your lips, tongue, gums, mouth and throat are injury free, you do not have bleeding or sores on your lips, tongue, gums, mouth or throat and if you don't perform oral sex on a woman while she is menstruating.

Unprotected intercourse between people of the opposite sex can lead to pregnancy. The use of condoms containing Nonoxynol-9 greatly reduces this risk. If you need more protection than this your local Planned Parenthood may be able to help with other alternatives.

If your condom breaks or if you think that seminal fluid has escaped, certain after-sex pills may be an option. Be sure to contact the 888-NOT-2-LATE emergency number within 24 hours to find out more about them.

Disclaimer:
The above information is compiled from various reference sources and the opinions of various organizations and individuals. It is designed to provide current and authoritative information on the subject matter covered. It is provided with the understanding that the publishers are not engaged in rendering medical, legal or other professional service. The authors of this information accept no responsibility or liability for any accident, injury, mishap or incident that may occur to any individual(s) or groups as a result of performing any of the activities described or alluded to herein. Every effort has been made to ensure that the enclosed information is correct, but this publication should not be considered a substitute for formal medical advice.

References, Resources and Additional Information:
The Society for Human Sexuality
The CDC's STD treatment guidelines
National STD Hotline
Planned Parenthood Center

Party Waiver

NOTE: This waiver has been successfully used in court by Club X, and with their permission, I have adapted it for use at My Dungeon parties.

AGREEMENT AND RELEASE OF LIABILITY

Voluntary Participation
1. I am at least 18 years of age and am freely and voluntarily choosing to attend and participate in this event and to view and/or participate in activities that I know are adult oriented and sexually explicit and that involve acts of domination, submission, bondage, discipline, sadism and masochism, and other explicit and extreme sexual fetishes and activities, including, but not limited to, spanking, paddling, whipping, waxing, piercing, fire play, knife or edge or blood play, bondage, suspension, fisting and other oral, vaginal and anal penetration. I understand that these activities involve certain risks, including, but not limited to, the possible negligent or reckless conduct of other participants. Initials: _____.

Assumption of Risk
2. I AM AWARE THAT THESE ACTIVITIES ARE CONSIDERED EXTREMELY HAZARDOUS ACTIVITIES. I AM VOLUNTARILY PARTICIPATING IN THESE ACTIVITIES WITH FULL KNOWLEDGE OF THE DANGERS INVOLVED, AND I ACCEPT AND I ASSUME FULL RESPONSIBILITY FOR ANY AND ALL RISKS OF PROPERTY DAMAGE, PERSONAL INJURY OR DEATH. I VERIFY THIS STATEMENT BY PLACING MY INITIALS HERE: _____.

Release
3. As consideration for being permitted to enter the event, and to view and participate in these activities, and to use the facilities and equipment being provided, I agree that neither I nor anyone through me or on my behalf will make any claim against or sue Bamm!, His! t or anyone affiliated with the Bamm! Clan,

including, but not limited to, his friends, associates, guests, agents, employees, employers, teammates, landlords, volunteers, promoters, sponsors and contractors, owners, lessors or suppliers of the premises, and the owners, lessors or suppliers of any equipment used in connection with the event, for any injury or damage suffered by me at any time during my presence at the event or as a result of my participation in any activities at the event, and I hereby release, waive and forever discharge them, their heirs, administrators, executors and assigns, from any and all claims, demands, actions or rights of action, of whatever kind or nature, either in law or in equity, arising from, or by reason of, my attendance at, or participation in, the event or activities. Initials: _____.

Indemnity and Hold Harmless

4. I agree to indemnify and hold harmless Bamm!, the Bamm! Clan and all those individuals and entities described in paragraph 3 above, from any loss, liability, injury, damage or cost that they may occur or that they may incur due to my presence or my actions at the event, whether caused by my negligence or otherwise. Initials_____.

Knowing and Voluntary Execution

5. I HAVE CAREFULLY READ THIS DOCUMENT AND I FULLY UNDERSTAND ITS CONTENTS. I AM AWARE THAT THIS IS A RELEASE OF LIABILITY AND A CONTRACT BETWEEN ME AND BAMM! AND THAT I AM GIVING UP MANY LEGAL RIGHTS AND REMEDIES BY SIGNING IT. Initials _____.

Printed Name_____

Signature_____ Date_____

Scene or screen name_____

House Party Rules

These are the rules that I use at My parties. Adapt them as necessary for your use.

All play shall be Consensual. No illegal substances of any kind are allowed on the premises. Firearms may not be brought into my home.

Prostitution, solicitation, and negotiation of compensation for sexual services ARE ILLEGAL and are not tolerated. Violations shall result in immediate removal and banning from future events. Scene professionals may not accept payment for any services rendered.

Normal scene etiquette is required (i.e., Do not interfere with a scene, do not invade scene space, etc). Please keep conversation, laughter and comments to a minimum in the play areas. Do not monopolize the equipment. Do NOT join a scene unless specifically asked to do so!

Please clean up after your scene. Leave all equipment free of sweat, blood, other bodily fluids, wax, toys, etc. Wax, fire, and scenes involving bodily fluids need to be performed in the area set aside for those purposes. Bodily fluids may include perspiration, blood, vaginal secretions, semen, urine, and other substances. Safer sex precautions are strongly encouraged, and all bodily fluids must be cleaned up upon completion of the scene. When in doubt, please ask the host or the DM on duty.

Cameras and other types of recording devices are NOT allowed without the expressed written permission of the host.

There is no smoking in the house. Smoking areas have been set aside for the smokers.

If you wish to drink alcohol, it's BYOB, but be sure to take it with you when you leave.

Penetration is acceptable. But please do so in designated body fluid areas, only.

Only the host(ess), or a designee of such, will open or unlock the front door. This is for the protection of the host(ess) and all the guests.

Honest, open, respectful negotiation is welcome. Nonconsensual play is not. You are expected to know that the other people here might ask you to play. There is a wide variety of play that is possible. In other words, please read and be familiar with our rules. The person who asks is expected to be polite, and to respect the collar of anyone who is collared, or to respect the relationships of other couples or leather families. If you want to play with the person who asks, you are welcome to say, "Yes." If you do not want to play with the other person, you are expected to say, "No." If you do not want to play with the other person, but say, "Yes," or do not safeword (if that is what is necessary to prevent unwanted play), then you have violated their trust. We have no mind readers. If you ask someone to play, and they say, "No," you are expected to respect their wishes, and to let the matter drop.

The DM will have unrestricted access to all areas of play space.

Disclaimer
Neither the management, owners, or operators of the event space, nor any agents, successors or assigns of any of the foregoing shall be held liable to any attendee, or any agents, successors or assigns of that attendee, for injury to person or property incurred as a result of attendance at this event. Participants by their attendance assume all risks of such attendance.

A Short Version of the submissive's Checklist

This is a shorter version of the checklist, which you should fill out and provide to your Top. This will provide a quick check to identifying limits, negotiating play and finding common ground. I amended the original checklist to give you a better idea of my interests.

For each item, you need to provide two answers:
For Experience, write YES or NO next to each item to indicate if you have ever DONE that activity. Mark N/A if it does not apply to you.
For Willingness, indicate for each item how you feel about DOING that activity by rating it on a scale of NO or 0 to 5.
"?" means you don't understand what the item is attempting to describe.
NO means you will NOT do that item under any circumstances (a hard limit).
0 (zero) indicates you have utterly no desire to do that activity and don't like doing it (in fact, may loath it) and would ordinarily object to doing it, but you would permit Me to do it if I really wanted to (sometimes called a "soft limit").
1 means you don't want to do, or like to do this activity, but wouldn't object if it was asked of you.
2 means you are willing to do this activity, but it has no special appeal for you.
3 means you usually like doing this activity, at least on an irregular/occasional basis.
4 means you like doing this activity, and would like to experience it on a regular basis.
5 means the activity is a wild turn-on for you, and you would like it as often as possible.
Mark with an asterisk (*) those items which you are willing to do only with your Top, but not with casual play-partners.
Write down any additional information which might be important to know to the right.

There is intentionally some overlap between activities. Unless otherwise stated, the sub is the recipient/target of the activity.

Activity	Y/N	N or 0-5
Anal sex		
Anal plugs		
Arm & leg sleeves (armbinders)		
Asphyxiation		
Beating (soft)		
Blindfolds		
Being serviced (sexual)		
Being bitten		
Bondage		
Breath control		
Bruises		
Caning		
Chains		
Chauffeuring (driving)		
Choking		
Chores (domestic service)		
Clothespins		
Cock worship		
Collars		
Corsets (wearing casually)		
Cuffs		
Cutting		
Dildoes		
Double penetration		
Examinations (physical)		
Exhibitionism		
Eye contact restrictions		
Face slapping		
Fantasy abandonment		
Fantasy rape		
Fantasy gang-rape		
Fear (being scared)		

Fisting (vaginal)
Following orders
Forced homosexuality
Forced heterosexuality
Forced masturbation
Forced nudity
Forced servitude
Forced sodomy
Full head hoods
Gags
Genital sex
Golden showers
Hair pulling
Hair or head held during oral sex
Hand jobs (giving)
Hand jobs (receiving)
Harems (serving w/other subs)
Harnessing
Head (give fellatio/cunnilingus)
Head (recv fellatio/cunnilingus)
High heel wearing
Hoods
Housework (doing)
Ice cubes
Immobilization
Kidnapping
Kneeling
Knife play
Leather clothing
Leather restraints
Lectures for misbehavior
Licking (non-sexual)
Lingerie (wearing)
Manacles & Irons
Manicures (giving)
Massage (giving)
Modeling for erotic photos

Mouth bits
Nipple clamps
Nipple play/"torture"
Oral/anal play (rimming)
Over-the-knee spanking
Orgasm control
Outdoor sex
Pain
Persona training (in scene)
Phone sex
Piercing (temporary, play-pierce)
Prison scenes
Prostitution scenes
Punishment scene
Pussy worship
Riding crops
Rituals
Restrictive rules on behavior
Scratching - getting
Sensory deprivation
Serving
Serving as furniture
Serving as a maid
Serving as waitress/waiter
Serving orally (sexual)
Serving other Doms
Shaving (body hair)
Shaving (genital hair)
Skinny-dipping
Slutty clothing
Spanking
Speech restrictions (when, what)
Spreader bars
Standing in corner
Stocks
Strait jackets
Strap-on-dildos (sucking on)

Strap-on-dildos (penetrated by)
Strap-on-dildos (wearing/using)
Suspension
Supplying new partners for Dom
Swallowing semen
Swapping/Swinging
Teasing/Tickling
Triple penetration
Uniforms
Verbal humiliation
Vibrator
Voyeurism (watching others)
Voyeurism (your Dom w/others)
Video (watching others)
Video (recordings of you)
Wearing symbolic jewelry
Whipping
Wooden paddle (punishment)

The End

I hope you've enjoyed this book and have learned a little bit more about What It Is That We Do. I've written the book in a pocket-sized format so that you can carry it with you as a reference and resource. Feel free to bend the page corners as needed; I promise not to scream. If you'd like me to do one of the presentations found within these pages, if you need a new Master, would like to schedule a book signing, or if you'd just like to chat for a while, feel free to shoot me an email at SirBamm@SirBamm.com.

But please give me more than a minute to get back to you before screaming that I'm a worthless POS who refuses to follow through with his promises and is not at all trust-worthy. I promise I will eventually answer all my emails.